Masturbation as a Means of Achieving Sexual Health

Masturbation as a Means of Achieving Sexual Health has been co-published simultaneously as *Journal of Psychology & Human Sexuality*, Volume 14, Numbers 2/3 2002.

The *Journal of Psychology & Human Sexuality* Monographic "Separates"

Below is a list of "separates," which in serials librarianship means a special issue simultaneously published as a special journal issue or double-issue *and* as a "separate" hardbound monograph. (This is a format which we also call a "DocuSerial.")

"Separates" are published because specialized libraries or professionals may wish to purchase a specific thematic issue by itself in a format which can be separately cataloged and shelved, as opposed to purchasing the journal on an on-going basis. Faculty members may also more easily consider a "separate" for classroom adoption.

"Separates" are carefully classified separately with the major book jobbers so that the journal tie-in can be noted on new book order slips to avoid duplicate purchasing.

You may wish to visit Haworth's website at . . .

http://www.HaworthPress.com

. . . to search our online catalog for complete tables of contents of these separates and related publications.

You may also call 1-800-HAWORTH (outside US/Canada: 607-722-5857), or Fax 1-800-895-0582 (outside US/Canada: 607-771-0012), or e-mail at:

getinfo@haworthpressinc.com

Masturbation as a Means of Achieving Sexual Health, edited by Walter O. Bockting, PhD, and Eli Coleman, PhD (Vol. 14, No. 2/3, 2002). *"Finally, here is an excellent book filled with research illustrating how positive attitudes toward masturbation in history, across cultures, and through-out the life span can help in the achievement of sexual health. This book is an invaluable re-source and I highly recommend it for all who are teaching health or sexuality education or are involved in sex counseling and therapy." (William R. Strayton, PhD, ThD, Professor and Coordinator, Human Sexuality Program, Widener University)*

Sex Offender Treatment: Accomplishments, Challenges, and Future Directions, edited by Michael H. Miner, PhD, and Eli Coleman, PhD (Vol. 13, No. 3/4, 2001). *An easy-to-read collection that reviews the major issues and findings on the past decade of research on and treatment of sex offenders. The busy professional will find this book A quick and helpful update for their practice. The reviews presented are succinct, but capture the main issues to be addressed by anyone working with sex offenders." (R. Langevin, PhD, CPsych, Director, Juniper Psychological Services and Associate Professor of Psychiatry, University of Toronto)*

Childhood Sexuality: Normal Sexual Behavior and Development, edited by Theo G. M. Sandfort, PhD, and Jany Rademakers, PhD (Vol. 12, No. 1/2, 2000). *"Important. . . . Gives voice to children about their own 'normal' sexual curiosities and desires, and about their behavior and development." (Gunter Schmidt, PhD, Professor, Department of Sex Research, University of Hamburg, Germany)*

Sexual Offender Treatment: Biopsychosocial Perspectives, edited by Eli Coleman, PhD, and Michael Miner, PhD (Vol. 10, No. 3, 2000). *"This guide delivers a diverse look at the complex and intriguing topic of normal child sexuality and the progress that is being made in this area of research."*

New International Directions in HIV Prevention for Gay and Bisexual Men, edited by Michael T. Wright, LICSW, B. R. Simon Rosser, PhD, MPH, and Onno de Zwart, MA (Vol. 10, No. 3/4, 1998). *"Performs a great service to HIV prevention research and health promotion. . . . It takes the words of gay and bisexual men seriously by locating men's sexual practice in their love relationships and casual sex encounters and examines their responses to HIV." (Susan Kippax, Associate Professor and Director, National Center in HIV Social Research, School of Behavioral Sciences, Macquarie University, New South Wales, Australia)*

Sexuality Education in Postsecondary and Professional Training Settings, edited by James W. Maddock (Vol. 9, No. 3/4, 1997). *"A diverse group of contributors–all experienced sexuality educators–offer summary information, critical commentary, thoughtful analysis, and projections of future trends in sexuality education in postsecondary settings. . . . The chapters present valuable resources, ranging from historical references to contemporary Web sites." (Adolescence)*

Walter O. Bockting
Eli Coleman
Editors

Masturbation as a Means of Achieving Sexual Health

Masturbation as a Means of Achieving Sexual Health has been co-published simultaneously as *Journal of Psychology & Human Sexuality*, Volume 14, Numbers 2/3 2002.

Pre-publication REVIEWS, COMMENTARIES, EVALUATIONS . . .

"Finally, here is an excellent book filled with research illustrating how positive attitudes toward masturbation in history, across cultures, and throughout the life span can help in the achievement of sexual health. This book is an invaluable resource and I highly recommend it for all who are teaching health or sexuality education or are involved in sex counseling and therapy."

William R. Strayton, PhD, ThD
*Professor and Coordinator,
Human Sexuality Program,
Widener University*

Sexual Coercion in Dating Relationships, edited by E. Sandra Byers and Lucia F. O'Sullivan (Vol. 8, No. 1/2, 1996). *"Tackles a big issue with the best tools presently available to social and health scientists. . . . Perhaps the most remarkable thing about these excellent chapters is the thread of optimism that remains despite the depressing topic. Each author. . . chips away at oppression and acknowledges the strength of women who have experienced sexual coercion while struggling to eliminate sexist assumptions that deny women sexual autonomy and pleasure." (Naomi B. McCormick, PhD, Professor, Department of Psychology, State University of New York at Plattsburgh)*

HIV/AIDS and Sexuality, edited by Michael W. Ross (Vol. 7, No. 1/2, 1995). *"An entire volume on the topic of HIV and sexuality, bringing together a number of essays and studies, which cover a wide range of relevant issues. It really is a relief to finally read some research and thoughts about sexual functioning and satisfaction in HIV-positive persons." (Association of Lesbian and Gay Psychologists)*

Gender Dysphoria: Interdisciplinary Approaches in Clinical Management, edited by Walter O. Bockting and Eli Coleman (Vol. 5, No. 4, 1993). *"A useful modern summary of the state-of-the-art endocrine and psychiatric approach to this important problem." (Stephen B. Levine, MD, Clinical Professor of Psychiatry, School of Medicine, Case Western Reserve University; Co-Director, Center for Marital and Sexual Health)*

Sexual Transmission of HIV Infection: Risk Reduction, Trauma, and Adaptation, edited by Lena Nilsson Schönnesson, PhD (Vol. 5, No. 1/2, 1992). *"This is an essential title for understanding how AIDS and HIV are perceived and treated in modern America." (The Bookwatch)*

John Money: A Tribute, edited by Eli Coleman (Vol. 4, No. 2, 1991). *"Original, provocative, and breaks new ground." (Science Books & Films)*

Masturbation as a Means of Achieving Sexual Health

Walter O. Bockting, PhD
Eli Coleman, PhD
Editors

Masturbation as a Means of Achieving Sexual Health has been co-published simultaneously as *Journal of Psychology & Human Sexuality*, Volume 14, Numbers 2/3 2002.

The Haworth Press, Inc.
New York • London • Oxford

Masturbation as a Means of Achieving Sexual Health has been co-published simultaneously as *Journal of Psychology & Human Sexuality™*, Volume 14, Numbers 2/3 2002.

The development, preparation, and publication of this work has been undertaken with great care. However, the publisher, employees, editors, and agents of The Haworth Press and all imprints of The Haworth Press, Inc., including The Haworth Medical Press® and Pharmaceutical Products Press®, are not responsible for any errors contained herein or for consequences that may ensue from use of materials or information contained in this work. Opinions expressed by the author(s) are not necessarily those of The Haworth Press, Inc. With regard to case studies, identities and circumstances of individuals discussed herein have been changed to protect confidentiality. Any resemblance to actual persons, living or dead, is entirely coincidental.

Cover design by

The Haworth Press, Inc., 10 Alice Street, Binghamton, NY 13904-1580 USA

Library of Congress Cataloging-in-Publication Data

Masturbation as a means of achieving sexual health / Walter Bockting, Eli Coleman, editors.
  p. cm.
  "Co-published simultaneously as Journal of psychology & human sexuality, Volume 14, Numbers 2/3 2002."
  Includes bibliographical references and index.
  ISBN 0-7890-2047-5 (hard : alk. paper) – ISBN 0-7890-2046-7 (pbk : alk. paper)
  1. Hygiene, Sexual. 2. Masturbation. I. Bockting, Walter O. II. Coleman, Eli. III. Journal of psychology & human sexuality.
RA788 .M338 2003
613.9'5–dc21
                            2002152624

Indexing, Abstracting & Website/Internet Coverage

This section provides you with a list of major indexing & abstracting services. That is to say, each service began covering this periodical during the year noted in the right column. Most Websites which are listed below have indicated that they will either post, disseminate, compile, archive, cite or alert their own Website users with research-based content from this work. (This list is as current as the copyright date of this publication.)

Abstracting, Website/Indexing Coverage . . . . Year When Coverage Began

- *Cambridge Scientific Abstracts (Risk Abstracts) <www.csa.com>* . . . 1992
- *CNPIEC Reference Guide: Chinese National Directory of Foreign Periodicals* 1995
- *Educational Administration Abstracts (EAA)* 1995
- *e-psyche, LLC <www.e-psyche.net>* 2002
- *Family & Society Studies Worldwide <www.nisc.com>* 1996
- *Family Violence & Sexual Assault Bulletin* 1991
- *FINDEX <www.publist.com>* 1999
- *Gay & Lesbian Abstracts <www.nisc.com>* 2000
- *GenderWatch <www.slinfo.com>* 1999
- *Higher Education Abstracts, providing the latest in research & theory in more than 140 major topics* 1991
- *HOMODOK/"Relevant" Bibliographic database, Documentation Centre for Gay & Lesbian Studies, University of Amsterdam (selective printed abstracts in "Homologie" and bibliographic computer databases covering cultural, historical, social and political aspects of gay & lesbian topics, % HOMODOK-ILGA Archive, OZ Achterburgual 185, NL-1012 DK Amsterdam, The Netherlands)* 2002

(continued)

*Special Bibliographic Notes related to special journal issues
(separates) and indexing/abstracting:*

- indexing/abstracting services in this list will also cover material in any "separate" that is co-published simultaneously with Haworth's special thematic journal issue or DocuSerial. Indexing/abstracting usually covers material at the article/chapter level.
- monographic co-editions are intended for either non-subscribers or libraries which intend to purchase a second copy for their circulating collections.
- monographic co-editions are reported to all jobbers/wholesalers/approval plans. The source journal is listed as the "series" to assist the prevention of duplicate purchasing in the same manner utilized for books-in-series.
- to facilitate user/access services all indexing/abstracting services are encouraged to utilize the co-indexing entry note indicated at the bottom of the first page of each article/chapter/contribution.
- this is intended to assist a library user of any reference tool (whether print, electronic, online, or CD-ROM) to locate the monographic version if the library has purchased this version but not a subscription to the source journal.
- individual articles/chapters in any Haworth publication are also available through the Haworth Document Delivery Service (HDDS).

Masturbation as a Means of Achieving Sexual Health

CONTENTS

ABOUT THE EDITORS

Walter Bockting, PhD, is a Licensed Psychologist and Assistant Professor at the Program in Human Sexuality, Department of Family Practice and Community Health, at the University of Minnesota Medical School in Minneapolis. He is also on the graduate faculty of the University's Center for Advanced Feminist Studies. Dr. Bockting is a native of The Netherlands and received his PhD from the Vrije Universiteit in Amsterdam. For the past 15 years, he has worked as a psychotherapist assisting clients with a large variety of sexual concerns. In addition, he teaches medical students, residents, and psychologists in human sexuality. His research interests include gender identity, HIV/STD prevention, and the promotion of sexual health. He has published and presented at many national and international scientific conferences on these topics. Dr. Bockting is the author of *Transgender HIV Prevention: A Minnesota Response to a Global Health Concern,* and editor of the *International Journal of Transgenderism, Gender Dysphoria: Interdisciplinary Approaches in Clinical Management* (The Haworth Press, Inc.), and *Transgender and HIV: Risks, Prevention, and Care* (The Haworth Press, Inc.). He is a member of the Board of Directors of the Harry Benjamin International Gender Dysphoria Association and a past president of the Midcontinent Region of the Society for the Scientific Study of Sexuality.

Eli Coleman, PhD, is Director of the Program in Human Sexuality (Department of Family Practice and Mental Health) at the University of Minnesota Medical School in Minneapolis. He is the author of numerous articles and books on sexual orientation, compulsive sexual behavior, sexual offenders, gender dysphoria, chemical dependency and family intimacy, and the psychological and pharmacological treatment of a variety of sexual dysfunctions and disorders. He is particularly noted for his research on pharmacotherapy in the treatment of compulsive sexual behavior and paraphilias. Dr. Coleman is the founding and current editor of the *Journal of Psychology in Human Sexuality* and the *International Journal of Transgenderism*. He is one of the past presidents of the of the Society for the Scientific Study of Sexuality, the current past president of the World Association for Sexology, and the current President of the Harry Benjamin International Gender Dysphoria Association. He has been the recipient of numerous awards, including the Surgeon General's Exemplary Service Award for outstanding support of the United States Surgeon General as a contributing Senior Scientist on the "Surgeon General's Call to Action to Promote Sexual Health and Responsible Sexual Behavior." He has also received the Richard J. Cross Award for Sexuality Education from the Robert Wood Johnson Medical School. Dr. Coleman was given the Distinguished Scientific Achievement Award from the Society for the Scientific Study of Sexuality in 2001 and the Alfred E. Kinsey Award for outstanding contributions to the field of sexology by the Midcontinent Region of the Society for the Scientific Study of Sexuality in 2002.

Introduction

Walter O. Bockting

Masturbation remains taboo, and this is not without consequences for the promotion of sexual health. When I was involved in establishing partnerships with community organizations targeting low-income African American women for HIV/STD prevention, a collaborative relationship was canceled specifically because we were planning to address masturbation and homosexuality in the intervention curriculum. I was not surprised about the controversial nature of homosexuality; after all, this topic continues to be contentious in many segments of society. However, perhaps in part because of my background as a native from The Netherlands, a country known for sexual tolerance and freedom, I was astounded to discover that discussing masturbation as part of promoting safer sex was deemed inappropriate. Moreover, while homosexuality has been studied extensively in the field of sexual science, masturbation has received remarkably little attention in sex research.

A few years later, when I was looking for a theme for the 1999 annual conference of the Midcontinent Region of the Society for the Scientific Study of Sexuality, Eli Coleman–co-editor of this volume–suggested the topic of masturbation. He had attempted to publish a special issue of the *Journal of Psychology & Human Sexuality* on this topic before but without success due to an insufficient number of submissions. Indeed, in her commentary on masturbation, Tiefer (1998) noted that masturbation was the most sensitive topic in the U.S. National Health and Social Life Survey, making both respondents and interviewers the most uncomfortable (Laumann, Gagnon, Michael, & Michaels, 1994). Tiefer

[Haworth co-indexing entry note]: "Introduction." Co-published simultaneously in *Journal of Psychology & Human Sexuality* (The Haworth Press, Inc.) Vol. 14, No. 2/3, 2002, pp. 1-4; and: *Masturbation as a Means of Achieving Sexual Health* (ed: Walter O. Bockting and Eli Coleman) The Haworth Press, Inc., 2002, pp. 1-4. Single or multiple copies of this article are available for a fee from The Haworth Document Delivery Service [1-800-HAWORTH 9:00 a.m. - 5:00 p.m. (EST). E-mail address: getinfo@haworthpressinc.com].

went on to argue that masturbation must be appreciated as a complex sexological issue, in need of research examining what masturbation means to different people at different points in their lives (Tiefer, 1998, p. 10). A scientific conference on masturbation would acknowledge masturbation as a key component of sexual health. It was our hope that such a conference would allow us to assess and share current knowledge on masturbation, stimulate research, and lead to the publication of selected papers that would make valuable contributions to the field.

Hosted by Richard Keeling at the University of Wisconsin in Madison, the conference brought together scientists from around the United States to discuss the study of masturbation. Focus of the presentations ranged from the role of masturbation in sexual development, its impact on relationships and spirituality, treatment of compulsive masturbation, and masturbation as a means to self-actualization, to the role of scientific knowledge about masturbation in public policy. Over the course of the three days of this conference, we learned that while masturbation is central to our understanding of human sexuality, science is very much in its infancy in developing a comprehensive research agenda into the subject. Few studies to date have gone beyond asking the basic questions of do you masturbate, if yes how often, and to what extent do you experience guilt. Meeting with colleagues from around the nation provided us with a forum where we could formulate the important questions to be asked about this significant yet neglected topic in sex research.

It should come as no surprise then that–even after this conference–compiling a publication to provide a broad discussion of research into masturbation proved challenging. We invited everyone who presented at the conference to submit a manuscript. In addition, we invited several other scientists in the field to contribute. The papers initially submitted, however, did not provide a sufficiently comprehensive discussion of the topic of masturbation. Just when we had decided to cancel the publication for this reason, additional research came to our attention resulting in new submissions able to round out and complete the issue. I thank Eli Coleman for his belief in this project, and Jakub Jedynak and Priscilla Palm for their assistance.

Eli Coleman introduces this volume with the synthesis he provided at the conclusion of the conference on Masturbation. He leads with his thesis that masturbation is a critical component in the development of sexual health, explores the power of masturbation (both positively and negatively), and outlines a number of viable ideas for future research.

Vern L. Bullough offers a historical overview of attitudes toward masturbation in a number of different cultures. Like most non-procreative sex, masturbation was long seen as sinful or pathological; it was not until the 20th century's new discoveries about sexually transmitted diseases that masturbation could be studied more objectively. Bullough argues that understanding attitudes toward masturbation is key to understanding societal attitudes toward human sexuality in general.

The two articles that follow report on empirical findings of changes in masturbatory behavior in the 20th century in Northern Europe. Shifts over time include earlier age of masturbation for especially women, and an increased recognition of masturbation as a source of sexual pleasure irrespective of other sexual activity or relationship status.

Bean E. Robinson and colleagues report on the relationship between masturbation and HIV risk as predicted by the Sexual Health Model among a sample of African American women. Contrary to expectations, results showed that participants who masturbate were more likely to have multiple partners, be in a nonmonogamous relationship, and engage in high-risk sexual behaviors. Next, Steven D. Pinkerton and colleagues report similar findings among a sample of college women: those who first masturbated at a younger age were at higher risk for HIV. In addition, a trend was found toward higher HIV risk for women who reported more frequent current masturbation. Both Robinson and Pinkerton conclude that among women, frequency of masturbation may be a good indicator of overall sexual interest. Greater sexual interest then can be expected to translate into more, but not necessarily safer, sexual behavior.

Finally, Brian D. Zamboni and Isiaah Crawford examine the relationship between masturbation and sexual fantasy, sexual desire, and dyadic sexual activity. Their findings confirm the impression of Robinson and Pinkerton that masturbation may be an indicator of overall sexual desire. Zamboni found that masturbatory desire and frequency have close relationships with sexual thoughts, fantasies, and dyadic sexual desire. They developed a model that suggests that (1) sexual thoughts and fantasies lead to masturbatory desire, which in turn leads to masturbation; (2) sexual fantasy influences dyadic sexual desire, which in turn influences dyadic sexual activity; and (3) masturbatory activity appears to influence dyadic sexual desire, which in turn influences dyadic sexual activity. This model supports the notion that masturbation may be useful in treating individuals with low sexual desire, a notion widely accepted among sex therapists but rarely tested empirically.

Because of the current scarcity of research on masturbation, this volume provides an important service as it offers examples and ideas for legitimate scientific inquiry into masturbation and sexual health. Tiefer's (1998) call still stands: sexology could benefit from a thorough exploration of the various meanings and contexts of masturbation with the promise of providing greater insight into all aspects of human sexuality. I hope that sexual scientists will step up their research on masturbation, a practice after all familiar to so many of us.

REFERENCES

Laumann, E. O., Gagnon, J. H., Michael, R. T., & Michaels, S. (1994). *The social organization of sexuality: Sexual practices in the United States*. Chicago, IL: University of Chicago Press.

Tiefer, L. (1998). Masturbation: Beyond caution, complacency and contradiction. *Journal of Sex and Marital Therapy, 13* (1), 9-14.

Masturbation as a Means
of Achieving Sexual Health

Eli Coleman, PhD

ABSTRACT. Research on masturbation has indicated that, contrary to traditional beliefs, masturbation has been found to be a common sexual behavior and linked to indicators of sexual health. While there are no general indicators of ill health associated with masturbation, it can be powerfully negative or positive for many individuals. As an example, it is widely used in sex therapy as a means of improving the sexual health of the individual and/or relationship. Promoting masturbation as a means of a public health strategy for sexual health is highly controversial; however, there are arguments and evidence that suggest that this may be an important part of any public health approach to improving sexual health. There is a need for more research on the impact of masturbation on self-esteem, body image, sexual functioning and sexual satisfaction and methods for using masturbation to promote sexual health. There is also a need for more of a theoretical approach to the formation of hypotheses to be tested. *[Article copies available for a fee from The Haworth Document Delivery Service: 1-800-HAWORTH. E-mail address: <getinfo@haworthpressinc.com> Website: <http://www.HaworthPress.com> © 2002 by The Haworth Press, Inc. All rights reserved.]*

Dr. Coleman is Professor and Director of the Program in Human Sexuality, Department of Family Practice and Community Health at the University of Minnesota Medical School. He can be contacted at: 1300 S. 2nd Street, Suite 180, Minneapolis, MN 55454 USA (E-mail: colem001@tc.umn.edu).

This paper was based upon a presentation at the 1999 Annual Meeting of the Midcontinent Region of the Society for the Scientific Study of Sexuality, Madison, Wisconsin, May 23, 1999.

[Haworth co-indexing entry note]: "Masturbation as a Means of Achieving Sexual Health." Coleman, Eli. Co-published simultaneously in *Journal of Psychology & Human Sexuality* (The Haworth Press, Inc.) Vol. 14, No. 2/3, 2002, pp. 5-16; and: *Masturbation as a Means of Achieving Sexual Health* (ed: Walter O. Bockting and Eli Coleman) The Haworth Press, Inc., 2002, pp. 5-16. Single or multiple copies of this article are available for a fee from The Haworth Document Delivery Service [1-800-HAWORTH 9:00 a.m. - 5:00 p.m. (EST). E-mail address: getinfo@haworthpressinc.com].

5

KEYWORDS. Masturbation, sexual health, sexual fantasies, sexual behavior

Over a half a century ago, Kinsey and his associates stunned the world with their research that indicated that masturbation was a common sexual activity and was apparently non-pathological. Ninety-two percent of the men in their sample reported having masturbated (Kinsey, Pomeroy & Martin, 1948). Their groundbreaking research began a series of studies which have continued to debunk many beliefs that were previously held by science and influenced cultural attitudes and practices. In a more recent survey of sexual behavior of individuals in the United States, 62% of men and 42% of the women reported that they had masturbated in the preceding year (Laumann, Gagnon, Michael, & Michaels, 1994). Today, it is now well recognized within science that the perceived ill-health effects of masturbation are mostly based upon ancient religious orthodoxy and mythology (Leitenberg, Greenwlad & Tarran, 1989; Money, Prakasam & Joshi, 1991).

In fact, research has indicated that masturbation begins early and seems to be an important part of healthy sexual development (Langfeldt, 1981). It is often a marker of sexual development (Bancroft, Herbenick, D., & Reynolds, 2002). Many learn about their bodies and sexual responsiveness with masturbation through adolescence and young adulthood (Atwood & Gagnon, 1987). Masturbation also continues throughout the life span. For example, many adults continue to masturbate even though they are married and have ready access to sexual intercourse (Laumann et al., 1994). It is also a safe alternative when there is a risk of a sexually transmitted infection, including HIV. Masturbation can also help older people who do not have an available partner to maintain sexual functioning and expression (Leiblum & Bachmann, 1988).

Masturbation has also been linked to orgasmic capacity, healthy sexual functioning and sexual satisfaction in relationships. For example, Kinsey found that women who had not experienced orgasm before marriage were much less likely to be orgasmic with their partners in marriage (Kinsey, Pomeroy, Martin & Gephard, 1953). Other research has found that married women who masturbated to orgasm had greater marital and sexual satisfaction than women who did not masturbate (Hurlburt & Whittaker, 1991). Among women, positive attitudes about sexuality and orgasmic capacity have been positively correlated to masturbation (Kelly, Strassberg & Kircher, 1990).

Masturbation has also been found to be a means of increasing comfort with one's body and self-esteem (Dodson, 1987). Comfort with one's body is essential to decrease anxiety in interpersonal sexual contexts, improve comfort with being sexual and increase sexual satisfaction (Barbach, 1976). Masturbation improves sexual satisfaction between partners during sexual activity together. It also relieves pressure for partners to be sexual only together. It provides a sexual outlet for individuals when their partners are disinterested in sex or are unavailable.

Consequently, sexual therapists have used masturbation as some of the first steps in treating sexual dysfunctions with success (LoPiccolo & Lobitz, 1972). The assumption has been that increasing self-knowledge about one's own sexual response is critical to teaching one's partner how to give pleasure to them. Masturbation has been a proven technique as part of treatment of sexual dysfunctions (Heiman, LoPiccolo, & LoPiccolo, 1976; Heiman & LoPiccolo, 1988; Zilbergeld, 1992; Leiblum & Rosen, 1989).

Limits to the Positive Aspects of Masturbation

While masturbation has been shown to be a healthy form of sexual expression and a means of improving sexual satisfaction and treating sexual dysfunctions, most of the ill effects of masturbation come from the guilt associated with the behavior and not the behavior itself. It can also cause problems because of the misunderstanding of the meaning of masturbation in interpersonal relationships (Hunt, 1974; Michael et al., 1994).

Masturbation can be associated with pathology as in the case of paraphilias and compulsive sexual behaviors. However, these are relatively rare sexual pathologies (Coleman, 1992). Any healthy sexual behavior can be taken to its obsessive and compulsive extreme and cause difficulty for the individual and/or interfere in interpersonal relationships (Money, 1986).

MASTURBATION REMAINS STIGMATIZED

Despite the scientific evidence indicating that masturbation is generally a normal variant of sexual expression and that it does not seem to have a causal relationship with sexual pathology, negative attitudes about masturbation persist and it remains stigmatized. While some religions are taking a more neutral stance, many religions of the world continue to condemn the practice (Nelson, 1979). Not surprisingly, parents are often uncomfortable and respond negatively to pre-adolescent masturbation (Gagnon, 1985). Masturbation continues to be a major source of anxiety for many individuals and couples.

THE CHALLENGE FOR SEXOLOGISTS

Most sexologists today continue to strive to eliminate myths and negative attitudes about masturbation. They do it through research, teaching, clinical practice, and community health initiatives. There is the basic task of "normalizing" masturbation. Many sexologists, however, are interested in going beyond reducing "unease" and trying to help people enjoy and feel pleasure during masturbation. Today, there is more concern about promoting joy, satisfaction, and pride about masturbation. But, these methodologies to promote joy, satisfaction and pride have not been well described in the literature nor are there studies examining their efficacy.

Overcoming the Barrier: The Threat to the Common Enterprise

There remain many barriers to normalizing and promoting positive attitudes about masturbation. First, there is the basic barrier that there is still a general stigma attached to sexual education. But, while there is a general anxiety about sexuality education, probably the most sensitive topics within sexuality education are masturbation, contraception and homosexuality. But what is unique about these topics that raises so much concern and doubt? John Gagnon (1999) has speculated that the major reason for this is because these activities are a threat to the common enterprise. They are a threat to the common enterprise because they involve non-procreative sex. Further, masturbation raises other concerns as well. The fact is that masturbation is self-focused and its main purpose is to give self-pleasure. This behavior violates the ethics of many societies that require sacrifice and work for the common good. Thus, masturbation is perceived to be too selfish and too pleasure focused for the common good.

The Power of Meaning of Masturbation

Consequently, masturbation takes on a power of meaning within individuals and society. It can be powerfully negative or positive, being determined by the interaction between the prevailing societal attitudes and individual attitudes and behaviors.

The Negative Power. Because of the stigma promoted by cultural and religious beliefs, masturbation has the power to create intense guilt and shame in individuals. It can also cause conflicts in relationships. This can lead to further problems in intra-personal and interpersonal functioning, sexual and mental disorders. Because of the stigma of masturbation promoted by many of the world's religions, this can contribute to spiritual alienation as well.

The Positive Power. Masturbation gives the individual the opportunity to learn about their body and sexual response. Because sexual pleasure is given to oneself, it has been speculated that it contributes to an individual's sense of ownership, control and autonomy over their own body. Bodily integrity is not only a sexual right but also a key ingredient in sexual health (World Association for Sexology, 1999). Contrary to the myth that masturbation would increase self-focus and selfishness, improved self-identity and self-esteem has been viewed as a critical ingredient for establishing intimacy with others. Therefore, masturbation can be a tool to improve one's capacity for intimacy with others. Because of the traditional stigma attached to masturbation by religions of the world, approaching masturbation through a more positive approach can facilitate spiritual connectedness. These are some of the key ingredients of sexual health (Robinson et al., 2000). Therefore, masturbation can be a pathway to increasing one's sexual comfort, satisfaction and overall health.

Masturbation as a Means of Promoting Sexual Health

Coleman (1997) outlined 10 steps for promoting sexual health. These included: providing comprehensive sexuality education; insuring education for health professionals; increasing research in child and adolescent sexuality; overcoming homophobia, biphobia and transphobia; ending sexual violence; promoting masturbation; promoting sexual functioning; creating better access to health care; and recognizing sexual health as a basic human right. While all of these steps were deemed critical, upon further analysis, some of the most critical steps would be overcoming homophobia, biphobia, and transphobia and the promotion of masturbation. Once completing these steps, it was reasoned that the other barriers to sexuality education, therapy and research would fall away. The reason that these two points were seen as so critical is because they do challenge the common enterprise and the concept of procreative sex. Much of the underlying fears of sexuality education and research is that sexologist will somehow validate these perceived threats. So, while controversial, Coleman (1997; 1999) specifically called for promoting masturbation as a means of promoting sexual health.

THE NEED FOR MORE RESEARCH AND ESTABLISHING A RESEARCH AGENDA

Much of the research on masturbation has asked the following questions: "Do you masturbate?" "How often?" "Do you feel guilty?" As research in this area continues, the questions need to go beyond these fundamental ones. There are several issues that need to be addressed. It is important to consider with whom do we study. Some studies have been conducted on small samples which are difficult to generalize from. Large epidemiological studies have been valuable to understand basic attitudes and practices. However, there are always problems of generalizing the results of these studies. We seem to be at a stage that we need to go beyond large epidemiological studies to understand the meaning, purpose and power of masturbation. In doing this, different methodologies need to be considered. The questions asked need to be carefully considered and it is important that they are age and culturally appropriate. If the questions are done in person, the training and the characteristics of the individuals need to be carefully considered.

While research has documented the links and correlations to sexual health, there is much more for us to understand in terms of the power of masturbation. Further, we need to understand how to minimize its negative effects and maximize its positive effects. This will take a greater systematic study of the phenomenon. And, we will need more of a multi-disciplinary approach to this investigation, including biological (neurophysiological and genitophysiological), psychological and sociological studies. In addition, we will need to learn from systematic analysis from history, art, and literature. We will need both quantitative and qualitative research. Some examples of the types of research which need to be conducted are discussed below.

In the quest for more research on masturbation, it is also clear that there needs to be more of a theoretical approach to the formation of hypotheses to be tested. While not exhaustive, there are a few theories that have the potential for developing greater understanding. For example, Bowlby (1969; 1971) asserts that psychological health is dependent upon a healthy balance between autonomy and attachment. There are developmental tasks that determine that healthy balance. Does masturbation contribute to a healthy establishment of autonomy? Will this greater autonomy contribute to an individual's capacity for attachment? Are individuals with a balance of autonomy and attachment more likely to have masturbated and found these experiences pleasurable and guilt free? Some of the research cited earlier in this paper has supported this notion, however, we need more research that will test these hypothesis based upon this theoretical framework.

Maslow (1988) has asserted that psychological health is dependent upon a person's ability to self-actualize. Does masturbation contribute to self-actualization? Some individuals describe masturbation in terms of peak experiences. Do masturbatory peak experiences contribute to self-actualization? Are people who are self-actualized more likely to have masturbated and found these experiences pleasurable and guilt free? There is some research that supports these notions, but it would be helpful to have more research designed that would be based upon the hypotheses generated from this theoretical framework.

Many individuals who masturbate are unlikely to discuss this with others. Is there a coming out process similar to that of gay and lesbian individuals? Are there stages of a coming out process that leads to integrating masturbation with overall identity? Are gay and lesbian individuals who have achieved integration (Coleman, 1982) or identity synthesis (Cass, 1979) more likely to have masturbated and experience their masturbatory experiences as pleasurable and affirming in contrast to individuals at earlier stages of coming out?

Understanding Differences in Masturbatory Attitudes and Experiences

We know there are significant gender differences. Males masturbate more than females. These differences have been attributed to male and female anatomy and physiology, as well as to socio-cultural influences. To what degree are these differences explained by biological explanations versus social-cultural influences? There are differences in racial/cultural groups, by socio-economic class, by education and by religious affiliation (Kinsey et al., 1948, 1953; Cortese, 1989). These differences certainly point to socio-cultural determinants but it is unclear how these determinants actually influence attitudes and behavior. The reasons for these differences have been highly speculative and need further exploration.

Some of these differences have been shown to be rather universal. For example, a number of studies have replicated the fact that males masturbate more than females (e.g., Hatano, 1991; Erkmen, Dilbaz, Serber, Kaptanolglu & Tekin, 1990; Alzate, 1989). In some cases, the differences are more dramatic in some cultures than others. This again points to the impact of socio-cultural factors. Consequently, an interesting line of research would be to track changes in attitudes and behaviors especially given the effects of acculturation, globalization and urbanization.

And, then there is the question of individual differences. Is there a genetic predisposition to greater interest in sexual expression, including masturbation (beyond the male/female differences)? We can best study these differences within the sexes. We know that there is great variability in onset of masturbatory activity in males and females. What influences these individual differences?

The Relationship Between Fantasy and Masturbation

Another line of research that would be very interesting to explore would be the relationship of fantasy to masturbation. The most common themes associated with masturbation are reliving a past sexual experience, sexual activity with one's current partner, sexual activity with an idealized partner, and same sex sexual activity. Other common fantasies involve oral sex, sex in a romantic setting, group sex, and forcing and being forced to have sexual activity (Leitenberg & Henning, 1995). While we know that forcing or forced sex fantasies are common sexual fantasies and seem unrelated to actually wanting to be involved in such activities, we know little about the meaning of these fantasies (Leitenberg & Henning, 1985). There are other uncommon fantasies that may shed more light on the meaning, purpose, and power of masturbation. Research in this area is sparse and, yet, these are important questions.

Another area that is in need of investigation is the question of under or overstimulation of fantasy material. With the advent of the Internet, access to erotica, fantasy stimulation, cybersex in all of its manifestations is rapidly expanding. We know very little how this is having an impact on people's sexuality. How does involvement with fantasy and masturbation on the Internet impact sexual health of individuals and how does it impact their partners? There is a myriad of questions. For example, people are having fantasized relationships which are quasi-real. Are these activities viewed as a violation of fidelity to one's partner if they know about these activities?

How does this stimulation impact on people's relationships? Does this facilitate interpersonal functioning or does it inhibit it? Are there some people that are more vulnerable to experience its potential negative effects? In extreme cases, there are people who have become compulsive about their Internet use, we can see the negative consequences in the clinical situation (Cooper, Scherer, Boies, & Gordon, 1999). However, how much is too much? If it interferes, how does it do so? Is the overstimulation of the media related to the epidemic of underaroused individuals with sexual desire disorders that we see in our clinics? Or is this simply a phenomenon that is explained by other factors. These are all interesting and important questions in need of informed responses.

The Effects of Comprehensive Sexuality Education

What are the effects of comprehensive sexuality education on attitudes and behaviors regarding masturbation? The research on sexuality education has tended to focus on age of onset of sexual activity with others, use of contraception, and condom usage. However, we need to study more the effects of comprehensive sexuality education which teaches about masturbation and its effects on self-esteem, body image, sexual development and sexual functioning within relationships.

Effects of Public Health Strategies to Promote Sexual Health

Is there a correlation between public health policy towards sexual health promotion and masturbatory attitudes and behavior? There are wide differences in ministries of health and education to develop policy and programs for sexual health promotion. The dangers of promoting masturbation are best illustrated by the fact that a recent Surgeon General of the United States was asked to resign by President Bill Clinton after a speech she gave in December of 1994 at the World AIDS Day Conference at the United Nations. She suggested that people ought to know about masturbation as one possible alternative to intercourse for the prevention of HIV. The statement was, "Masturbation is a part of human sexuality, and it's a part of something that perhaps should be taught. But we have not even taught our children the basics. And I feel that we have tried ignorance for a long time and its time we try education." (Elders, 1994). We have recently seen efforts to develop these strategies on national and regional levels (Pan American Health Organization, 2000; U.S. Surgeon General, 2001). Most of these strategies advocate for more sexuality education, access to counseling and sexual health services and increased research. Will these initiatives produce changes in attitudes and behaviors regarding masturbation?

CONCLUSION

Human sexual expression is very diverse and there are many forms of sexual expression. The sexual health of an individual or society is enriched with the understanding, tolerance and compassion for the diversity of sexual expressions that are a part of the human condition. Human beings engage in many sexual activities that have no other purpose than to feel pleasure. Too many people experience guilt and shame over their sexuality because they perceive that they deviate from the expected societal norm. One of the sexual behaviors that have the power to produce pleasure and healthy sexuality or to induce guilt and shame and sexual pathology is masturbation. Sexology can play an important part in helping individuals find a means of enjoying the positive power of masturbation and minimizing the negative aspects. However, in order to inform the public, we need more research in this area. This will mean overcoming the stigma of researching the topic. Several research questions have been proposed in this paper and it is hoped that this will stimulate further research in this area.

REFERENCES

Alzate, H. (1989). Sexual behavior of unmarried Colombian university students: A follow-up. *Archives of Sexual Behavior, 18*, 239-250.

Atwood, J. D. & Gagnon, J. (1992). Mastubatory behavior in college youth. *Journal of Sex Education and Therapy, 13*, 35-42.

Bancroft, J., Herbenick, D., and Reynolds, M. (2002). Masturbation as a marker of sexual development. In Bancroft, J. (Ed.), Sexual *development*. Bloomington, IN: Indiana University Press.

Barbach, L. (1976). *For yourself: The fulfillment of female sexuality.* Garden City, NY: Doubleday.

Bowlby, J. (1969). Attachment, Vol. 1 of Attachment and loss. London: Hogarth Press. New York: Basic Books; Harmondsworth: Penguin (1971).

Cass, V. E. Cass, V. (1979). Homosexual identity formation: A theoretical model. *Journal of Homosexuality, 4* (3), 219-235.

Coleman, E. (1982). Developmental stages of the coming out process. *American Behavioral Scientist, 25*, 469-482.

Coleman, E. (1992). Is your patient suffering from compulsive sexual behavior? *Psychiatric Annals, 22* (6), 320-325.

Coleman, E. (1997). Promoting Sexual Health: The Challenges of the Present and Future. In J.J. Borras Valls & Conchillo, M.P. (Ed.), *Sexuality and Human Rights.* Valencia, Spain: Instituto de Sexologia y Psicoterapia, (pp. 25-35).

Coleman, E. (1999). Revolutionary changes in sexuality in the new millenium: Sexual health, diversity, and sexual health. In Cooper, A., Scherer, C.R., Boies, S.C., & Gordon, B. (1999). Sexuality on the internet: From sexual exploration to pathological expression. *Professional Psychology Research and Practice, 30* (2), 154-164.

Cortese, A. (1989). Subcultural differences in human sexuality: Race, ethnicity and social class. In K. McKinney & S. Sprecher (Eds.), *Human Sexuality: The Societal and Interpersonal Context.* Norwood, NJ: Ablex.

Dodson, B. (1987). *Sex for one. The joy of self love.* Glendale, CA: Crown.

Elders, J. (1994). Address to the World AIDS Day Conference at the United Nations.

Erkmen, H., Dilbaz, N., Serber, G., Kaptanoglu, C. & Tekin, D. (1990). Sexual attitudes of Turkish university students. *Journal of Sex Education and Therapy, 16*, 251-261.

Gagnon, J. (1985). Attitudes and responses of parents to pre-adolescent masturbation. *Archives of Sexual Behavior, 14* (5), 451-466.

Gagnon, J. (1999). Talk at Midcontinent Region. 1999 Annual Meeting of the Midcontinent Region of the Society for the Scientific Study of Sexuality, Madison, Wisconsin, May 21, 1999.

Hatano, Y. (1991). Changes in the sexual activities of Japanese youth. *Journal of Sex Education and Therapy, 17*, 1-14.

Heiman, J., LoPiccolo, L., & LoPiccolo, J. (1976). *Becoming orgasmic: A sexual growth program for women.* Englewood Cliffs, NJ: Prentice Hall.

Heiman, J. & LoPiccolo, J. (1988). *Becoming Orgasmic: A Sexual and Personal Growth Program for Women.* Englewood Cliff, NJ: Prentice Hall.

Hurlburt, D. & Whittaker, K. (1991). The role of masturbation in marital and sexual satisfaction: A comparative study of female masturbators and nonmasturbators. *Journal of Sex Education and Therapy, 17*, 272-282.

Hunt, M. (1974). *Sexual Behavior in the 1970's.* Chicago: Playboy Press.

Kelly, M. P., Strassberg, D. S., & Kircher, J. R. (1990). Attitudinal and experiential correlates of anogasmia. *Archives of Sexual Behavior, 19* (2), 165-167.

Kinsey, A., Pomeroy, W., & Martin, C. (1948). *Sexual behavior in the human male.* Philadelphia: W. B. Saunders.

Kinsey, A., Pomeroy, W. Martin, C. & Gephard, P. (1953). *Sexual behavior in the human female.* Philadelphia: W. B. Saunders.

Langfeldt, T. (1981). Childhood masturbation. In. L. L. Constantine & F. M. Martinson (Eds.), *Children and Sex* (pp. 63-74). Boston: Little Brown.

Laumann, E. O., Gagnon, J. H., Michael, R. T. & Michaels, S. (1994). *The social organization of sexuality: Sexual practices in the United States.* Chicago: University of Chicago Press.

Leiblum, S. & Rosen, R. C. (1989). *Principles and practices of sex therapy (2nd ed.).* New York: Guilford.

Leiblum, S. & Backmann, G. (1988). The sexuality of the climacteric woman. In B. Eskin (Ed.), *The Menopause: Comprehensive Management.* New York: Yearbook Medical Publications.

Leitenberg, H., Greenwald, E. & Tarran, M. (1989). The relationship between sexual activity among children during preadolescence and/or early adolescence and sexual behavior and sexual adjustment in young adulthood. *Archives of Sexual Behavior, 18,* 299-313.

Leitenberg, H. & Henning, K. (1995). Sexual fantasy. *Psychological Bulliten, 117,* 469-496.

LoPiccolo, J. & Lobitz, W. C. (1972). The role of masturbation in the treatment of orgasmic dysfunction. *Archives of Sexual Behavior, 2,* 163-171.

Maslow. A. (1988). *Toward a Psychology of Being (3rd Ed.).* New York: Wiley.

Michael, R., Gagnon, J., Laumann, E. & Kolaa, G. (1994). Sex in America. Boston: Little, Brown and Company.

Money, J. (1986). *Lovemaps: Clinical concepts of sexual/erotic health and pathology, paraphilia, and gender transposition in childhood, adolescence, and maturity.* New York: Irvington Publishers.

Money, J., Prakasam, K. S. & Joshi, V. N. (1991). Semen conservation doctrine from ancient Ayurvedic to modern sexological theory. *American Journal of Psychotherapy, 45,* 9-13.

Nelson, J. B. (1979). Embodiment: An approach to sexuality and christian theology. Minneapolis, MN: Augsburg Books.

Pan American Health Organization, Regional Office of the World Health Organization. (2000). The Promotion of Sexual Health: Recommendations for Action. Washington, D. C.: Author. Available in English and Spanish at: <*www.paho. org/English/HCP/HCA/PromotionSexualHealth.pdf*>;   <*www.paho.org/Spanish/ HCP/HCA/salud_sexual.pdf*>.

Robinson, B. R., Bockting, W. O., Rosser, B. R. S., Miner, M., & Coleman, E. (2001). The sexual health model: Application of a sexological approach to HIV prevention. *Health Education Research: Theory & Practice,* in press.

U. S. Surgeon General. (2001). The Surgeon General's Call To Action To Promote Sexual Health and Responsible Sexual Behavior. Washington, D.C. Author.

Zilbergeld, B. (1992). *The new male sexuality.* New York: Bantam Books. World Association for Sexology. (1999). Declaration of Sexual Rights. Available at: <*www.tc.umn.edu/nlhome/m201/colem001/was/*>.

Masturbation:
A Historical Overview

Vern L. Bullough, PhD, RN

ABSTRACT. The paper emphasizes that ideas about masturbation are cru-
cial to understanding any societal attitudes toward sex. It examines attitudes
to masturbation in ancient Egypt, Tigris Euphrates Valley, India, and
China. It looks at Biblical views and their misinterpretations and at the
Greek and Roman descriptions of masturbatory practices. Key to the development of western attitudes was the Augustinian version of sex which
was influenced by Augustine's personal background in Manichaeanism, a
religion which was based on ancient Persian beliefs. The Augustinian
view of all non-procreative sex as a sin was carried over into medicine in
the eighteenth century which changed sins into pathologies. The only ad-
vantage this had over the sin model (which still remained for large segments of the population) was that it allowed research to challenge past
assumptions and as medical ideas changed so did those about sex. It was
not until the beginning of the twentieth century with new scientific discoveries about sexually transmitted diseases that masturbation could be studied more objectively. Attitudes were slow to change but as they did so
attitudes towards human sexuality also changed. The two changes, it is
held, are closely tied together and this is why an understanding of attitudes toward masturbation is a key to understanding changing development in attitudes toward human sexuality. *[Article copies available for a fee
from The Haworth Document Delivery Service: 1-800-HAWORTH. E-mail address:
<getinfo@haworthpressinc.com> Website: <http://www.HaworthPress.com> © 2002 by
The Haworth Press, Inc. All rights reserved.]*

Vern L. Bullough is Adjunct Professor, University of Southern California, 3394 West
Sierra Dr., Westlake Village, CA 91362.

[Haworth co-indexing entry note]: "Masturbation: A Historical Overview." Bullough, Vern L. Co-published simultaneously in *Journal of Psychology & Human Sexuality* (The Haworth Press, Inc.) Vol. 14, No.
2/3, 2002, pp. 17-33; and: *Masturbation as a Means of Achieving Sexual Health* (ed: Walter O. Bockting and
Eli Coleman) The Haworth Press, Inc., 2002, pp. 17-33. Single or multiple copies of this article are available
for a fee from The Haworth Document Delivery Service [1-800-HAWORTH 9:00 a.m. - 5:00 p.m. (EST).
E-mail address: getinfo@haworthpressinc.com].

KEYWORDS. Masturbation, history, cultural assumptions, medicine

MASTURBATION

Masturbation is as old as the first humans but it remains a subject little researched and often misunderstood. Few forms of sexual activity have been as frequently discussed, so often condemned, and yet so universally practiced. So strong has been the hostility in western Christian culture to masturbation that even the linguistic roots of the word masturbation itself were distorted to emphasize its association with defiling oneself. Most western writers claimed the word was formed from a combination of the Latin word *manus* meaning hand with the word *stupro*, meaning to defile, thereby giving a stigma to the practice. This root for the word is a highly unlikely possibility since it implies the Romans were hostile to the practice which they were not, and there is a much simpler and less judgmental explanation. That is, the word *manus* was combined with the word *turbo*, to agitate or disturb, which would be far more descriptive of what takes place in masturbation, agitating by hand. The attempt to equate it with defiling is an editorial attempt to make an evil of the practice as well as many others since masturbation, in history, has often been used as a catchall term for a variety of sexual behaviors from *coitus interruptus* to same sex activities to the use of contraceptives.

Masturbation in Early Civilizations

For those who look for it, masturbation in spite of the ambivalence often expressed about it seems to have been ever present. Pictorial representations of the practice exist from preliterate cultures and references to it can be found in the earliest of writings. Mention of it, for example, occurs in the Pyramid Texts dating from the fifth and sixth Egyptian dynasties in the third millennium. In Egyptian mythology, the god Atum was said to have created the Ennead (a group of gods) by masturbating. Frequently, the male gods of Egypt are reported as masturbating in order to arouse themselves although there is little reported about the female gods, perhaps because the male element was regarded as the most important in biological terms. The male factor in generation was decisive, so decisive that it was believed possible that the gods even occasionally procreated without a female partner, but simply by masturbating (Bullough, 1976, pp. 61-62).

In the Tigris-Euprhates valley, masturbation is less discussed but the issue of male potency was of much concern. Males–having trouble with an erection–are urged to rub their penis or have it rubbed with a special oil to gain arousal. Masturbation seems to have been accepted and practiced and the erect penis was an important symbol. Stone models of them have survived in great quantity (Bullough, 1976, pp. 55-56). There is no information about female masturbation that has so far come to light in the Babylonian sources.

The ancient Hebrews were influenced by both Egyptian and the Babylonian tradition but it was in Judaism that the concept of uncleanliness came to be associated with masturbation. Any emission of semen outside the vagina, voluntarily or otherwise, was held to be a major source of contamination and required a purification ceremony.

> And if the flow of seed go out from a man, then he shall bathe all his flesh in water, and be unclean until the evening. And every garment, and every skin, whereon is the flow of the seed, shall be washed with water, and be unclean until the evening. (*Leviticus* 15: 16-17).

Uncleanness, however, is not restricted to masturbation since the writer adds that the woman also with whom a man shall lie carnally, shall both bathe themselves in water and be unclean until evening (*Leviticus,* 15: 18). This passage seems to imply that masturbation is not any more unclean an activity than copulation itself.

Moreover, uncleanness is not necessarily a violation of any moral code but rather a ceremonial one, and, therefore, is a lesser sin. This distinction was often ignored by later commentators, particularly Christian ones. The hostility to masturbation was so great that any and every scriptural reference was interpreted in the most negative terms. This was particularly true of the interpretation of the story of Onan, the son of Judah. According to the scriptures, Onan was struck dead by Jehovah for refusing to follow the Levirate custom of impregnating his dead brother's wife and instead resorted to "spilling his seed on the ground" (*Genesis* 38: 7-10). This was regarded by those Christian commentators hostile to masturbation as indicating that Jehovah regarded masturbation with such horror that its practitioners should be struck dead. Most scriptural scholars today argue the punishment was not for practicing *coitus interruptus* but for refusing to obey God's commandment about taking his brother's wife as his own. Unfortunately, since it is not always clear what the scriptural references mean, the sin of Onan became so equated with masturbation that Onanism became another term for autoeroticism. This is not to say that there was not Jewish opposition to masturbation and some commentators in the *Talmud* rigidly interdicted the practice. One even went so far as to regard masturbation as a crime deserving the death penalty. Others were far more tolerant but the loss of semen was troubling to most and it is within the realm of possibility that the Talmudic injunction against a man holding his penis even while urinating, except in the case of a married man whose wife was readily available for intercourse, resulted from the fear of the loss of semen (*Niddah* 13A, 1948).[2]

Why the loss of semen was so feared is unclear. It is possible that a loss was regarded as a failure of the male's duty to procreate and replenish the earth. But this simplistic answer is contradicted by the fact that it was permissible for women to use contraceptive measures and a common practice was the insertion of *mokh* (a spongy substance) into their vaginas to hinder conception (Yebamoth, 12b, 100b; Ketuboth, 39a; Niddah, 45a et al., 1948). Obviously the Hebrew writers regarded the male semen as the key to conception, but since not every act of intercourse, even under the most desirable conditions, resulted in pregnancy, procreation was not regarded as the sole purpose of sexual relations. In fact, a husband was supposed to have regular intercourse with his wife, even after the menopause. It is the uncleanness of masturbation which seems to be mostly emphasized but this then is no different from any other sexual activity. Still, one can see considerable ambivalence in the Jewish writings on the topic.

The permissive or at times ambivalent attitudes of the ancient near eastern civilizations, were challenged in the sixth and fifth centuries (B. C. E.) by the conquering Persians who brought with them their new dualistic religion of Zoroastrianism. The prophet Zoroaster emphasized that a sound body was essential to the maintenance of life in this generation and in future ones, and to gain such a body it was essential to control the desires of the flesh. Sex was necessary for procreation, but all aspects of sexual activity detracting from this purpose were to be condemned and prohibited, and this included masturbation (Bullough, 1976, p. 68). In fact, masturbation was regarded as one of the more heinous of activities since it did not lead to procreation, a view picked up by later religions in the west.

The belief that the male semen was precious and should be conserved was a common thread in other religions, although it did not necessarily result in a condemnation of masturbation. In Hinduism, *The Laws of Manu* stated:

Let him always sleep alone, let him never waste his manhood; for he who voluntarily wastes his manhood, breaks his vow. A twice-born student, who has involuntarily wasted his manly strength during sleep, must bathe, worship the sun, and afterwards thrice mutter the Rik-verse . . . (Müller, 1964, XI, 172)

Such discipline, however, generally was restricted to those who had sworn to observe a life of chastity. Other Hindus who engaged in masturbatory practices were only encouraged to make a light penance. In many of antinomian (pleasure seeking) sects or cults of Hinduism, however, masturbation became a religious ceremony associated with the god Krishna, who practiced manual orgasm. Indian women were often taught to give a deep massage to their daughters, as a purifying gesture, and same was true for male infants. The importance of self stimulation is evident in the number of artificial aids or dildos preserved from ancient times. Men were encouraged by writers of Hindu erotic manuals to stimulate their wife by dildos of various kinds before intercourse. Fixed stone *linga* or penises were located in a secluded part of many temples for girls and virgins to use in ritual defloration and for other purposes (Bullough, 1976, 163-64).

In ancient China, masturbation, particularly for males, was believed to result in a loss of vital essence. It was, however, condoned in special circumstances, such as when males, particularly young ones at the height of their *yang* were deprived of female companionship. The build up of undelivered sperm, it was believed, would block the whole system unless it was removed. Manipulation of the genitals was always encouraged but emission of semen was to be avoided. Even involuntary emissions were viewed with concern for they would diminish a man's vital force unless he compensated by acquiring an equivalent amount of *yin* essence from a woman. If male masturbation was either disapproved or tolerated under special circumstances, female masturbation, if not actively encouraged, was tolerated or ignored. It was feared that women who did not regularly have intercourse with ordinary mortals, might be forced to have intercourse with a devil. To avoid this, it was permissible for them to masturbate. There were many devices on the market to help from Ben wei balls to be inserted into the vagina to all kinds of dildos (Bullough, 1976).

THE CLASSICAL TRADITION

The ambivalence or even silence of the sources about masturbatory practices for women in the ancient sources remains less true for the Greco-Roman world. Women, in the minds of some classical medical and scientific authorities, needed to masturbate to stay sane. One of the characters in a Platonic dialogue describes a popular belief about the womb:

> [It was an] indwelling creature desirous of child-bearing. [When] it remains barren too long after puberty, it is distressed and sorely disturbed, and straying about in the body and cutting off the passages of the breath, it impedes respiration and brings the sufferer into extreme anguish and provokes all manners of diseases besides. (Plato, *Timaeus*, 1961, 91C)

While most of the classical medical writers rejected the idea of a wandering womb, the need for females to have orgasms remained a popular belief. Galen (second century C. E.), the dominant medical authority of the Roman empire, while rejecting outright the notion of a wandering womb, held that the womb had a biological desire to be pregnant and if there was no opportunity for intercourse, the woman would suffer. He taught that females produced a secretion in the uterus, similar to male semen, and the retention of which led to spoiling and corruption of the blood and subsequently to hysteria. To avoid such consequences, he proposed a remedy. First he applied warm compressors to the labia and then he used his fingers to masturbate the client:

> Following the warmth of the remedies and arising from the touch of the genital organs required by the treatment there followed twitchings accompanied at the same time by pain and pleasure after which she emitted turbid and abundant sperm. Thus it seems to me that the retention of sperm impregnated with evil essences had–in causing damage throughout the body–a much greater power than that of the retention of the menses. (Bullough, 1976, p. 10)

It was this explanation which percolated throughout the medieval and early modern period entering into male folklore as a belief that most female complaints could be cured by a good screwing. Galen, however, clearly advised masturbation as a cure. We know that Greek women masturbated with artificial phalluses and even rubbed each other's genitals. One of the Greek terms for a lesbian is *tribad* which means to rub.

Males quite clearly engaged in masturbation as well, some of it mutual or homoerotic, and there seemed to be little condemnation of it. Diogenes, the famed cynic, for example, was a masturbator. He reportedly said, afer being observed doing it, that "I wish to heaven I could in the same way satisfy my stomach with friction when it barks for food" (Diogenes Laertius, 1946, VI, 2, 46). Aristophanes in the *Wasps* (1949) has one of his characters says, "Yes, I will nurse him and get him all that is wanted for an old man: beef broth to lap, soft wool, and rug to keep him warm, and a courtesan to rub his member and his loins" (735-38).

In classical culture, if Rome is any example, masturbation was associated with the left hand. The Latin term for left is "*sinister*," a word which today has the connotation of evil, although this connotation was not necessarily due to the hand's use in masturbation, since the left hand was also associated with defecation. Moreover, from the Latin sources, we know that occasionally the right hand was used for masturbation or touching of the genitals or other purposes usually conducted in private. Interestingly, some individuals who masturbated preferred to use their right hand. Still, the epigrammist Martial (died about 104 M. E) makes numerous references to masturbation and left handedness:

> Oftentimes, Lygd, you swear you will grant my prayer, even appointing the place, even appointing the hour. Longtime I lay consumed with longing, till often my left hand comes to help in your stead. (Martial, 1968, XI, 74)

About himself Martial says, "Another Ganymede, my hand assisted me" (Martial, 1968, II, 43) or "Often my left hand comes to my help in your stead" (Martial, 1968, XI, 74). Sometimes the references seem hostile to the practice as in another epigram of Martial:

> Ponticus, you never enter a woman, but use your left hand as a mistress in Venus; do you think this is nothing? It is wrong-doing, believe me, indeed one so great that your own mind hardly grasps it. To be sure, Horatius copulated only once to beget triplets, Mars only once to get chaste Ilia with twins. Neither could have done it if by masturbation they had entrusted their dirty joys to their hand. You had better believe that Nature says to you, "What you are losing between your fingers, Ponticus, is a human being." (Martial, 1968, IX, xli)

The poet Catullus (first century B. C. E.) also speaks somewhat negatively of masturbation in his poems about Gellius. He reports that Gellius "practised gymnastic fornication" upon himself with his head lowered and in his spare time kept fingering his penis, "one reason" why "Gellius was lean" (Catullus, 1956, 88, 89).

The symbol of Priapus, the Roman god of fertility, was the erect phallus. His statutes were found almost eveywhere and women even wore little phalluses in a necklace. There is a collection of sayings entitled *Priapeia* in which the god himself reports on his own masturbation: "You see this organ after which I am called by my name Priapus, is wet, this moisture is not dew, nor yet hoarfrost. It is the outcome given of its own set will, on recalling memories of a complaisant maid" (*Priapeia*, 1937, XLVIII).

The nineteenth century compiler of classical erotica, Frederick Charles Forberg (1964) devoted a whole chapter to masturbation, and includes references to some hard to find illustrations. Among the authors he cites, in addition to those cited above are Juvenal, Ovid, Seneca, Herodotus, Pliny, and Valerius Maximus. In short, the Latin references to masturbation are multitudinous; and mostly favorable.

CHRISTIAN AND WESTERN ATTITUDES

With this background, the developing Christian Church had a variety of potential attitudes toward masturbation, and in fact the early Christians themselves had different attitudes. By the fourth century there were more than 200 separate Christian groups and although there was but one Jesus, there were many Christs. Each group of believers emphasized different views on a variety of topics encompassing almost every attitude present in the classical world. Although there were attempts to achieve a Christian unity at the Council of Nicaea in 325 M. E., a time when the Roman Empire adopted Christianity, the attempt failed. The rivalries continued, as the Church Councils declared more and more groups to be heretical. Many disappeared, some were severely persecuted, while others grew into important and long lived groups, many of them still with us. Christian unity was more of an ideal than a reality and each major group of Christians looked to different church fathers for their interpretations, although some of the earliest ones were common to all. The major formulator of western Christian attitudes on sexual issues is St. Augustine (354-430 M. E.) who gathered together an amalgam of scriptures and classical philosophical concepts to develop the theological foundation for the western Christian Church.

Augustine, before he had become a Christian, had been a Manichaean, a religion which combined some of the dualism of Zoroastrianism with elements of Christianity and Gnosticism.

Particularly strong in Manichaeanism was the association of sex with the weakness of the body. The Manichaeans deplored the earthly material body and exalted the spiritual and asexual aspect of the human soul. Augustine, a convert to Manichaeanism as a young man, strove mightily to achieve the prerequisite abstention from sex required of the true believer. Unfortunately, for him, he was obsessed by his sexual drives, and among other failing had a mistress and a son. We know a lot about his sex desires, perhaps the modern term might be compulsions, because he wrote an autobiography, entitled *Confessions,* in which he recounts how he prayed to God to save him from his sexual sins, but always with sort of crossed fingers and an implied saying, save me god but not yet. Ultimately, unable to meet the Manichaean demand for celibacy, he went through a crisis which resulted in his conversion to Christianity, whereupon he found he had lost his sexual desires and could live a celibate and chaste life (Augustine, 1919). In spite of his conversion, he still retained some of his Manichaean beliefs about the evils of sex, although he could not totally condemn sex with all those begats in the Bible and the appearance of Jesus at a marriage feast. He, however, held that the only permissible purpose of sex was as a procreative activity. He went even further and limited sex to face to face contact with the female on the bottom, the male on the top, and with the penis in the vagina. Any other kind of sexual activity was forbidden and sinful as was the use of any barriers to conception. Masturbation was forbidden. Although Augustine recognized that not every male (he wrote primarily in male terms) could find a wife or have the income to support one, his solution was not masturbation but a tolerance of prostitution, as a necessary evil. Without prostitution the men would turn to homosexuality, masturbation, and other more sinful activities (Bullough, 1976).

Inevitably, masturbation was regarded by medieval authorities as sinful not only because of the Augustinian arguments but also because it was widely believed (incorrectly) that animals did not engage in these practices, and thus it was an unnatural act. Inevitably, especially with the rise of monasticism and Christian asceticism in the fourth and fifth centuries, masturbation and sexual fantasies, conscious or unconscious, came to be regarded as serious moral problems. Lapses from the rule of sexual abstinence required that penances be performed, and a large number of early penitential manuals were written to guide members on what was permitted. Originally the manuals were designed to be used by the monastic authorities but their use spread to the secular church even though confession itself did not formally become a required ritual of the Medieval Church until the thirteenth century. Even involuntary nocturnal emissions indicated a moral lapse, and required the confessed sinner to stand for three successive nights for an hour long vigil. Adult masturbators in some of the early penitentials had to do penance for a year while a boy of twelve only had to do penance for 40 days (Bullough, 1976, p. 358). Interestingly, for a time, there was a somewhat lessening of the hostility to masturbation, and solitary masturbation came to be regarded by many as one of the least serious of sexual sins. Not all agreed, however, and there was always a contingent of theological writers such as the eleventh century Peter Damian who held that solitary masturbation was a type of sodomy and it, therefore, deserved all of the severe punishments visited on sodomists. Few of his immediate contemporaries agreed with him and as canon law developed in the twelfth century, masturbation required confession and penance but it was not a criminal offense only a moral one (Brundage, 1987, p. 214). If an orgasm was deliberately induced, however, there was a higher degree of guilt than if it happened accidentally. Interestingly, if a woman ruptured her hymen during masturbation or foreplay, she could still be counted as a virgin for ecclesiastical purposes unless penetration had actually occurred.

Towards the end of the Medieval period, masturbation again came under a more serious censure. In the generation after 1348 (the onset of the Black Death), there was concerted efforts to punish sodomists harshly. Unfortunately, sodomy was not always narrowly defined as sex between males but following the long deceased Peter Damian included anything considered "unnatural," including masturbation, mutual masturbation, oral sex, and anal sex, heterosexual or homosexual. Florence created a special magistrate court to deal with sodomy as did Venice, and anonymous denunciations were solicited (Brundage, 1987, p. 533).

The Catholic Church, following the development of Protestantism, continued to give prominence to the evils of masturbation, emphasizing its relationship to sodomy, and held those who practiced deserving of severe penalties although none of the authorities went quite so far as to prescribe the death penalty for it. Even a spontaneous orgasm, where no conscious self-stimulation was involved, was held to be morally wrong. One authority advised a person not engaged in marital sexual intercourse who felt a sexual climax coming on, to lie still, taking care to avoid touching the genitals, make the sign of the cross, and fervently pray beseeching God not to allow him or her to slip into orgasmic pleasure (Brundage, 1987, p. 571). Sex, outside of the missionary position in marital intercourse, was somehow impure, and if pleasure resulted from it, it was highly immoral and was to be avoided. Marital intercourse became a duty and any who felt pleasure from it were encouraged to feel guilty about it.

In general, the Protestants almost unanimously criticized the treatment of marriages and sex offences by the Catholic Church courts. Most held that ecclesiastical tribunals should have no jurisdiction over marriage at all, and increasingly, even in Catholic countries, princely and municipal courts extended their jurisdiction over offenses against sexual morality. Marriage law and ecclesiastical courts either ceased to exist on the continent or restricted themselves to settling disputes involving church property and similar matters. This was less true in England than elsewhere and there much of sexual behavior remained in control of ecclesiastical courts. Even in secular law, however, much of ecclesiastical belief persisted, and it was given a new force by developments in medicine. It was the medical model which developed in the seventeenth and eighteenth century which gave "scientific" data for proof of the dangers of masturbation, just as the power of religious authorities was waning, that raised the fear and dangers of masturbation to new heights.

MEDICAL AUTHORITIES AND MASTURBATION

In general, ancient and medieval medical writers had been somewhat tolerant of masturbation and sexual activity, and in fact generally believed that regular sexual intercourse was essential for health. Galen, the dominant medical authority for much of the western world, had held that people needed sexual relief and compared it to the need for bowel movements and urination. Though medieval medical authorities respected Galen's teachings, they often found themselves troubled by the resulting conflict between the demands of health and morals. Many of them simply tried to avoid confrontation on the issue and dealt with it only in passing although not necessarily harshly.

Although Galen remained influential well into the modern era, some of the new theories in medicine which developed in the seventeenth and eighteenth centuries, challenged his ideas about sexual activity in general, and masturbation in particular. Much of this new medical theorizing was due to the need for physicians to come up with diagnoses and treatments at a time when some of the ancient ideas were being challenged but before bacteriology and the germ theory of disease developed. Common to most of the theories was a concept of homeostasis, that is health and well-being was the normal state of the body, and illness occurred when the homeostasis broke down. Disease was little more than the tendency of nature to reestablish the normal order of tonic movements as quickly and efficiently as possible. The living body was composed of fibers having a special characteristic–*tonus*. When tonus functioned normally, the body was healthy, but every modification of it brought about a disturbance of health. Each theoretician had a slightly different concept but particularly vulnerable in most of the theories was the nervous system, and sexual activity came to be regarded as requiring an expenditure of great nervous energy. The great Dutch physician Hermann Boerhaave (1688-1738) had become particularly concerned with the effects of the loss of semen on the body. He concluded from observation and case studies that a rash expenditure of semen brought on a lassitude, a feebleness, a weakening of motion, fits, wasting, dryness, fevers, aching of the cerebral membranes, obscuring of the senses, and above all the eyes, a decay of the spinal chord, a fatuity, and other like evils. Others joined in (see Bullough, 1976, pp. 496-99) but particularly influential was the Swiss physician, S. A. D. Tissot, who labeled all non-procreative sexual activity as onanism (Tissot, 1766).

The dangers of masturbation that Tissot and others wrote about were portrayed in very graphic terms, leading to increasing public concern, and what in retrospect seems to be a panic response eventually resulting in what has been called the age of "masturbatory insanity." One reason for the fear was the increasing awareness of the dangers of sexually transmitted diseases, particularly gonorrhea and syphilis which, for a time in the eighteenth century, were regarded as different manifestations of the same disease. This confusion of the two was compounded by the fact that it was not realized that syphilis had three stages. Though it became clear at the end of the nineteenth century that the third stage, which was often delayed for years, could attack the heart, the brain, the spinal cord, and various other parts of the body, these sequellae earlier were thought to be due to sex activity itself. A hyperactive sex life posed such a strain on the nervous system that all kinds of degeneration occurred. Particularly dangerous was any form of non-procreative sex, especially masturbation which threatened the very existence of the human species.

But there was other "evidence" as well as the observations based on what we now know as venereal diseases. Patients in the emerging mental institutions were observed to be continually masturbating and it was believed by many "authorities" that the strain on their nervous system caused by such actions was what had caused them to go insane. Undoubtedly, masturbation filled the time of people confined with other mentally ill and mentally compromised person, and with little to do, and who were not inhibited by societal sanctions against auto-eroticism. Tissot, in six points, summed up the dangers. Onanism (all non-procreative sex), he said, led to (1) cloudiness of ideas and sometimes even madness; (2) decay of bodily powers, resulting in coughs, fevers, and consumption; (3) acute pains in the head, rheumatic pains, and an aching numbness; (4) pimples of the face, suppurating blisters on the nose, breast, and thighs, and painful itchings; (5) eventual weakening of the power of generation as indicated by impotence, premature ejaculation, gonorrhea, priapism, and tumors in the bladder; and (6) disordering of the intestines, resulting in constipation, hemorrhoids, and so forth.

Americans through the influence of the great Benjamin Rush, a signer of the Declaration of Independence, and one of the premier American physicians of the time, signed on to the "modern science" and widely publicized the medical concern with the dangers of masturbation. He warned his fellow citizens against careless indulgences in sex which could only result in "seminal weakness, impotence, dysury, tabes dorsalis, pulmonary consumption, dyspepsia, dimness of sight, vertigo, epilepsy, hypochondriasis, loss of memory, manalgia, fatuity, and death." Rush did not entirely discount the postive aspects of sex, and he argued that abnormal restraints on sexual activity were dangerous. It was masturbation which had to be controlled (Rush, 1794-98).

The nineteenth century saw a virtual flood of literature against masturbation from a great variety of "authorities," including individuals like Sylvester Graham, inventor of Graham crackers, John Harvey Kellogg, associated with his brother in the breakfast food cereal industry. Both male and female writers condemned it. Elizabeth Osgood Goodrich Willard, an early feminist, held that the sexual orgasm was more debilitating to the system than a day's work. She regarded sex as more or less a loathsome thing and was unhappy that people were generated under a system so easily abused. Any abnormal action was abuse (Willard, 1867). There were popular books telling parents how to recognize the signs of masturbation in their children and a parent in reading them would find that almost any conduct or behavior children and teenagers engaged in as sure signs of masturbation. Yet the consequences of such behaviors were so dangerous that it was necessary for parents to control it. Parents, for their part, were frantic about the dangers that children might suffer if they masturbated and sought advice from the "experts" on ways to stop them from doing so. Some physicians perforated the foreskin of the penis and inserted a ring or cut the foreskin with jagged scissors, making it painful to rub it. Some advised applying a hot iron to the clitoris and scarring it to prevent masturbation. Some simply burned the girl's thighs. Others applied ointments to the genital area that made the genital tender to touch. In some cases clitoridectomies were performed, labias sometimes cut out, and in males castration was sometimes done; in a few extreme cases actual amputation of the penis was attempted to prevent masturbation. A practice posing such horrendous dangers, demanded heroic treatment (Bullough, 1995, pp. 67-94). Obviously only a small minority of physicians and parents resorted to the most drastic measures, but large numbers of people turned to devices of one sort or another to curtail the ill effects of masturbation. Dozens and dozens of mechanical devices are listed under the category of medical appliances in the U. S. patent office records. Many were designed to fit over the penis in some way or other so that the wearer could not touch it; some of the devices had prickly points or metal teeth on the inside designed to make any erection in the male extremely painful. For girls, small baskets with wire screens were designed to fit over the vulva, through which they could urinate but were prevented from touching themselves. Many had locking devices in the back. Occasionally some of these appear in antique stores and are erroneously labeled as chastity belts. They were designed to prevent masturbation and date from the nineteenth and early twentieth century not the Middle Ages. There were special gloves that were put on children or others at night to prevent them from touching their genitals. There was even a device to prevent bed covers from coming into contact with sensitive areas (Bullough, 1987). One of the more lasting "cures" was the introduction of circumcision for boys so the child caretaker would not have to carefully pull back the foreskin in order to keep the penis clean. The justification for this was that it prevented the build up of smegma and this was an essential hygenic improvement on nature. Mothers certainly had to spend less time cleaning their infant boys. The debate over circumcision still goes on, long after most of society no longer accepts the belief in the dangers of masturbation that led to its adoption. Customs and practices are difficult to change.

HOW DID CONCEPTS CHANGE

Several factors worked to finally lessen the hysteria. Probably ultimately the most important was the development of the germ theory of disease and the discovery of the gonococcus causing gonorrhea and the spirochete causing syphilis at the end of the nineteenth century. By the end of the century also, the three stages of syphilis had been recognized and it was finally accepted that it was not simply an active sex life or the loss of semen through masturbation which led to illness but bacteria (and later viruses). Change, however, was slow and though Havelock Ellis at the beginning of the twentieth century challenged the myths of masturbation, many still continued to believe. Ellis's major contribution was to document that masturbation had been found among people of nearly every race, regardless of the condition in which they lived (Ellis, 1936). So strong was the negative cultural attitudes toward masturbation, that even Ellis still remained somewhat fearful of the consequences of excessive masturbation.

The fear of masturbation did have some fortuitous consequences for sex research. In 1915, Max Exner, a YMCA physician, concerned about masturbation and sex education, conducted one of the first surveys of sexual behavior in the United States, surveying nearly 700 college men about their sex practices. While his questionnaire was heavily biased against any sexual activity except that taking place in marriage, he found that masturbation was a common non-procreative sex activity. Initially he felt the only way to deal with this was to encourage the growth of sexual education designed to show young men how wrong they were, but eventually he came to the conclusion that a lot more research was needed to demonstrate this. His recognition of the need for serious research was one of the sparks which led to the Rockefeller supported Committee for Research in the Problems of Sex, the committee which ultimately funded Alfred Kinsey (Bullough, 1994). Incidentally, Exner later changed his mind about many of the dangers of masturbation.

By 1929 Ralcy Husted Bell, a physician, could state that:

> masturbation, by every known law of nature, according to clinical data, according to the plainest commonsense . . . is not more harmful than the co-operative act between mates. Why should it be? Certainly, if it were, the race would have destroyed itself ages and ages ago. The act, as a physiological function, is not in any sense an outlaw, physiologically considered. (Bell, 1932, p. 35)

In sum, masturbation was undoubtedly widely practiced in the past, often with tremendous guilt attached to it, and many individuals went through great anxiety about it, and not a few were mutilated or punished for it. Since the consequences of masturbation depended more on a mindset than any data, all kind of evil could be attributed to it. The germ theory challenged the assumptions behind the fear and anxiety about it, but it was only when modern sex researchers seriously began to investigate it in the twentieth century, that the great cloud surrounding it began to dissipate. Unfortunately, not everyone is aware of what we now know, and a lot of superstition still remains. Even an American surgeon general could be fired for speaking in favor of masturbation in the Clinton administration.

It is only by coming to terms with the history of western attitudes of masturbation, that we can begin to realize just how much of our traditional attitudes toward sex were based on erroneous conceptions and why serious discussion of masturbation must remain a central issue in any discussion of sexuality. If we can bring people to recognize that past "western" knowledge about masturbation was not only erroneous but worse, one that raised tremendous guilt feelings and insecurities about all sexual activity, they might be much more willing to look at sexuality as part of the normal makeup of human beings, something that many still have difficulty in accepting.

NOTES

Many of the sources for this paper are referenced in what historians call secondary sources rather than primary ones. This is because the APA style is not conducive to such citation, and the reader interested in pursuing the primary source, can turn to the cited secondary source for more detailed references.

1. For this and subsequent translations, I have relied on the edotion of the scriptures published by the Jewish Publication Society of America. The Christian version is slightly different and the verse numbers occasionally vary.

2. For Talmudic references, I have relied upon the English translations in the *Babylonian Talmud*, (1948f.) edited by I. Epstein, London: Soncino Press.

REFERENCES

Aristophanes (1949). *The Wasps*. Reprinted London: J. M. Dent.

Augustine (1919) *Confessions*, trans by William Watts. London: William Heinemann.

Bell, Ralcy H. (1932). *Self Amusement and Its Spectres*. Reprinted New York: Big Dollar Books.

Brundage, James (1987). *Law, Sex, and Christian Society in Medieval Europe* (Chicago: University of Chicago Press.

Bullough, V. L. (1976). *Sexual Variance in Society and History.* Chicago: University of Chicago Press.

Bullough, V. L. (1987). Technology for the Prevention of *"Les Maladies Produite par la masturbation."* *Technology and Culture* 28, pp. 828-32.

Bullough, V. L. (1994) *Science in the Bedroom.* New York: Basic Books.

Bullough, V. L. (1995). *Sexual Attitudes: Myths and Realities.* Buffalo: Prometheus Books.

Catullus (1956). *The Poems,* translated by Horace Gregory. New York: Grove Press.

Diogenes Laertius (1950). *Lives of Eminent Philosophers,* ed. and trans. R. D. Hicks. London: Heinemann.

Ellis, Havelock (1936). "Auto-Erotocism," part I, *Studies in the Psychology of Sex.* 2 vols., reprinted New York: Random House.

Forberg, Frederick Charles (1964). *De figuris veneris.* Reprinted New York: Medical Press.

Martial (1968). *Epigrams.* Ed. and trans. W. C. A. Ker. London: William Heinemann.

Müller, M.F. (1964). *Sacred Books of the East,* ed. Reprinted: Delhi: Motilala Banarsidass.

Plato (1961). *Timaeus.,* ed. and trans. R. G. Bury. London: William Heinemann.

Priapeia: An Anthology of Poems on Priapus. (1937). Ed. and translated by Michael S. Buck. Privately Printed.

Rush, Benjamin (1794-98). *Medical Inquires and Observations.* 5 vols., Philadelphia: Dobson.

Tissot, S. A. D. (1766). *Onanism: Or a Treatise upon the Disorders of Masturbation.* Trans. A. Hume. London: J. Pridden.

Willard, Mrs. E. O. G. (1867). *Sexology as the Philosophy of Life.* Chicago: J. R. Walsh.

Patterns of Masturbatory Behaviour:
Changes Between the Sixties
and the Nineties

Arne Dekker, Dipl. Soz.
Gunter Schmidt, PhD

ABSTRACT. In 1966, 1981 and 1996 the Department of Sex Research at Hamburg University, Germany, carried out three surveys into the sexual behavior of university students. Taken as a longitudinal study they provide information on the social history of sexuality over the past three decades for well-educated young adults (20 to 30 years old) in Germany. The samples consist of 8,641 men and women. In this paper data from the studies is analyzed under two aspects:

1. *Shifts in masturbatory behavior 1966-1981-1996.* Men and especially women begin to masturbate considerably earlier than used to be in the eighties, not to mention in the sixties. As a consequence, most young women nowadays have already experienced masturbation when having their first heterosexual intercourse–thus following a pattern of sexual socialization that traditionally was typical for boys. In addition, in 1996,

Arne Dekker is a sociologist (Dipl. Soz.) and conducts dissertation research on "construction of body and gender in virtual environments" at the Department for Sex Research at Hamburg University. Gunter Schmidt is Professor in this Department.

Address correspondence to Arne Dekker, Abteilung für Sexualforschung, Klinik für Psychiatrie und Psychotherapie, Universitaet Hamburg, Martinistrasse 52, D-20246 Hamburg, Germany (E-mail: arne_dekker@public.uni-hamburg.de).

This research was supported by grants from the Deutsche Forschungsgemeinschaft (Schm 261/5-1).

[Haworth co-indexing entry note]: "Patterns of Masturbatory Behaviour: Changes Between the Sixties and the Nineties." Dekker, Arne and Gunter Schmidt. Co-published simultaneously in *Journal of Psychology & Human Sexuality* (The Haworth Press, Inc.) Vol. 14, No. 2/3, 2002, pp. 35-48; and: *Masturbation as a Means of Achieving Sexual Health* (ed: Walter O. Bockting and Eli Coleman) The Haworth Press, Inc., 2002, pp. 35-48. Single or multiple copies of this article are available for a fee from The Haworth Document Delivery Service [1-800-HAWORTH 9:00 a.m. - 5:00 p.m. (EST). E-mail address: getinfo@haworthpressinc.com].

35

more students of both sexes had masturbated in the year preceding the investigation. The more relevant point is, however, that young adults (according to active incidence during the last 12 months) now masturbate almost irrespective of whether they have intercourse often or rarely, whether they are singles or live in a steady relationship or whether or not they are satisfied with their current relationship. So masturbation peacefully coexists with sex between partners and a loving relationship more often than it did in 1981 and 1966.

2. *Masturbation in steady relationships, 1996.* A detailed analysis of masturbation frequencies during the last four weeks also shows small differences between students who live in a sexually satisfying relationship and those without relationship. Only a minority feels the need to justify masturbation on the grounds that they lack sex with their partner. Three-quarters expressly state that masturbation is a form of sex in its own right and, therefore, does not interfere with partner sex. Furthermore, there is a tendency that students living in steady relationships experience masturbation slightly more positively than those living alone. *[Article copies available for a fee from The Haworth Document Delivery Service: 1-800-HAWORTH. E-mail address: <getinfo@haworthpressinc. com> Website: <http://www.HaworthPress.com> © 2002 by The Haworth Press, Inc. All rights reserved.]*

KEYWORDS. Sexual behaviour, masturbation, gender differences, social change of sexual behaviour

In their book "Sexual Conduct" published in 1973, William Simon and John Gagnon emphasised the important role masturbation plays in the sexual socialisation of adolescents: "The key role of the presence or absence of early sexual activity . . . cannot be underestimated in the reinforcing of a divergence in gender development" (p. 56). Above all, they stressed that due to their different attitudes towards masturbating, boys and girls grow up with differing sexual fantasies that generate long-term sexual scripts. "The key difference between males and females is that for the latter the organizing experience of puberty is the encouraging and furthering of the reality of marriage rather than, as for the former, the reality of sexual activity" (p. 56). These assumptions were supported by Kinsey's data collected during the forties (Kinsey et al. 1948, 1953; Gebhard and Johnson 1979).

The aim of this study was to discover whether male and female attitudes towards masturbation and actual behaviour still differ so widely, or whether as in many other areas of sexual behaviour (cf., Clement et al. 1984; Schmidt et al. 1998; Matthiessen 1999; Schmidt 2000)) the gap between them has gradually decreased. Although masturbation is no longer widely condemned thanks to increasingly liberal attitudes towards sex in recent years, the subject of sexual self-gratification still seems to be taboo even in the sex-friendly media of late modern society. This may be one reason why in most recent sex research projects (cf., Laumann et al. 1994; Johnson et al. 1994: Spira et al. 1994) little data has been collected on masturbation.

Drawing on the data provided by three investigations into the sexual behaviour of male and female students in Germany, our first concern here is whether there have been any changes in masturbatory behaviour over the periods 1966-1981-1996. As we will show, there have been two marked shifts: on the one hand masturbation has become more frequent and on the other hand people tend to enter into steady partnerships earlier than they used to. This leads us to look into a second point: the role masturbation plays in these steady relationships, using data from our latest investigation (1996) which is far more detailed than in the previous ones.

METHOD

Over the past thirty years the Department of Sex Research in Hamburg has undertaken three surveys into the sexual behaviour of male and female students at intervals of fifteen years, in 1966, 1981 and 1996 (Schmidt & Sigusch 1971, 1972; Clement et al. 1984; Schmidt et al. 1998; Schmidt 2000). A comparison of these three reports provides a wealth of information on the social history of the sex lives of this social group. Each investigation was based on a questionnaire sent to the students by regular mail. This contained between 300 and 400 questions; answering them took on average about one hour. All three investigations covered students from between 12 and 15 universities that were representative for German universities in terms of size, location, subjects offered and size of town. The questionnaire was sent to a random sample of students at each of these universities.

Figure 1 shows the size of the samples and the response rates. Altogether the three investigations comprised just over eight and a half thousand men and women who completed a questionnaire. Over the past

FIGURE 1. Size and Response Rates of Student Samples

	1966	1981	1996
Mailed questionnaires			
total	6,128	5,356	7,420
Samples			
men (n)	2,835	1,106	1,575
women (n)	831	816	1,478
total (n)	3,666	1,922	3,053
% women	23%	43%	48%
Response rate			
men	61%	33%	37%
women	55%	40%	47%
total	60%	37%	41%

thirty years the number of female students has doubled. While this figure largely mirrors the real shifts in the proportion of men and women at the universities, it also reflects our finding that in 1966 the women tended to refuse to participate more often than men, whereas in 1981 and 1996 the men were more reticent. The response rate, i.e., the number of filled-out questionnaires returned to us, was highest in 1966 at 60% and only about 40% in 1981 and 1996. This number is nevertheless an acceptable figure for sociological research. We have shown elsewhere (Schmidt et al. 1998, pp. 159-160; Schmidt 2000, pp. 24-29) that despite of the refusal rates our sample differs only slightly from the entire student population as far as major demographic variables are concerned. We, therefore, feel justified in assuming that our data provide an adequate representation of student sexuality, with unusual forms of sexual behaviour or relationships–both restrictive and expansive ones–slightly underrepresented.

The 1996 investigation partly covers the same ground as the older ones but only about 20% of the questions are identical. Therefore, only a few basic facts on masturbation can be compared over time; we lack any material from the first two investigations to compare with the responses to our questions in 1996 on masturbation within steady relationships. Since the average age of the students has risen continuously over the past thirty years, we have to restrict the comparison with previous investigations to the 20- to 30-year-olds. We also excluded data provided by students in East Germany who were studied only in 1996.

Our analysis of masturbatory habits in steady relationships in 1996, however, does include the 19- to 32-year-olds from both East and West Germany.

SHIFTS IN MASTURBATORY BEHAVIOUR 1966-1981-1996

A first sign that masturbation has gained new significance can be detected in the incidence of "age at first masturbation." In 1996 both genders begin markedly earlier than they did in the eighties, and much earlier than in the sixties (Figure 2).

One noticeable finding is that nowadays women tend to masturbate much earlier than their predecessors did. This shift means that most women have masturbated before they have their first intercourse–a pattern that used to be typically male (Figure 3).

The shifts in the differences between men and women's masturbation habits during adolescence become particularly obvious when one compares our data with Kinsey's college students, as is shown in Figure 4 on masturbation before the age of 20. The correlation between gender and

FIGURE 2. Age at First Masturbation (Accumulative Incidence) (%)

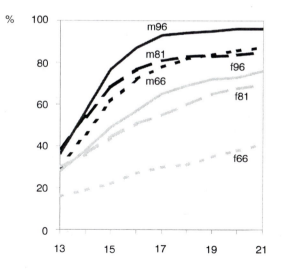

FIGURE 3. First Masturbation Before First Coitus (%)*

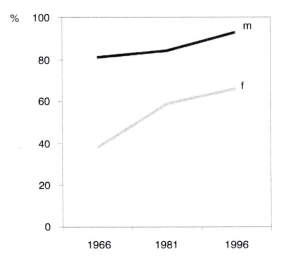

* Students with coital experience at age 19 or earlier only

FIGURE 4. Masturbation Before the Age of 20 (%)

	Men	Women	phi*
Kinsey	90	28	.65
1966	84	35	.50
1981	83	65	.21
1996	95	72	.31

*phi-coefficient gender x experience

masturbation decreased considerably between the forties and the eighties.

As well as starting earlier, in 1996 more students of both genders report masturbating during the last 12 months than their predecessors did. Interestingly this holds true for all subgroups according to partner status, quality of relationship and coital frequency (Figure 5). Overall, 94% of the men and 74% of the women report having masturbated during the previous 12 months. All these figures together suggest that mas-

FIGURE 5. Incidence of Masturbation in the Last 12 Months for Different Groups (%)

	Men			Women		
	'66	'81	'96	'66	'81	'96
All students	77	80	94	37	65	74
Steady relationship						
no steady relationship	86	81	97	39	71	76
relationship, 1-2 years	-	83	89	-	67	74
relationship, 3 years or more	72	77	92	43	63	71
Quality of relationship						
"I feel very good"	-	78	92	-	62	71
"I don't feel very good"	-	82	96	-	64	79
Monthly frequency of coitus						
0	81	77	94	31	59	60
6 and more	68	78	94	36	64	74
Sexual preferences						
heterosexual	-	79	94	-	64	74
bi- or homosexual	-	97	100	-	83	79

turbation is losing its stigma as a substitute for "the real thing" for both genders. It is acquiring a new status as a separate form of sex behaviour in its own right which is regularly resorted to even where having sex with a partner is part of normal life. It seems worth taking a closer look at how this peaceful coexistence between masturbation and partner sex functions.

MASTURBATION IN STEADY RELATIONSHIPS 1996

Focusing on how often the students masturbated in the four weeks preceding the study in 1996, here too one can only detect slight variations between the various groups. For both men and women the incidence remained more or less constant irrespective of whether they lived in a satisfying steady relationship or had neither a partner nor intercourse (Figure 6). Here, too, it appears that masturbation does not serve as a form of compensation for the lack of satisfying partner sex but is practised for its own sake by both men and women. The only differences lay in how frequently they masturbated; the men in particular did so less often the more intimate and satisfying the partnership (Figure 7).

FIGURE 6. Incidence of Masturbation in Past 4 Weeks in Different Groups (1996)

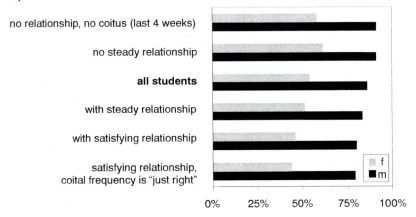

FIGURE 7. Monthly Frequency (Means) of Masturbation in Different Groups (1996)

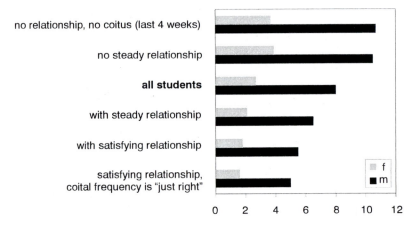

This brings us to another, remarkable finding. Quantitative sex research has consistently come up with evidence that the longer a partnership lasts the less intercourse the partners are likely to have (Johnson et al. 1994). Does this reduction in partner sex necessarily mean that the incidence of masturbation rises? Our data suggest that this is not the case. While in our sample intercourse is less frequent for those in a longer relationship, the frequency of masturbation appears to be stable over time (Figure 8).

In light of these findings the male and female student's attitudes to masturbation become easily intelligible: around three quarters of them emphasise that it is "a form of sex in its own right." Asked about their

FIGURE 8. Frequency (Means) of Coitus and Masturbation in the Past 4 Weeks, by Duration of Relationship (1996)

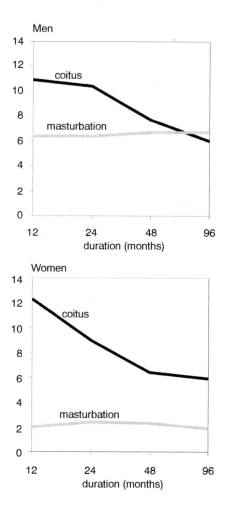

motives when masturbating last, 50-60% of those in steady relationships stated "I just felt like it," rather than "we couldn't have sex together" (Figure 9). Here too there are signs of a new approach to masturbation as a freely available, self-determined form of sex that is not bound up in the complications and demands of partner sex.

Do those who have a steady partner nevertheless feel differently about masturbating than singles do? Less than one in ten men and women had a bad conscience after masturbating, somewhat more of those living in a steady relationship than those living single. Apart from this result we found that men and women students living in steady partnerships were even slightly more positively inclined towards masturbation than those who lived alone (Figure 10).

Incidentally, there was little difference between the reports the students gave on their most recent masturbation and their most recent coitus–at least as far as the sexual pleasure involved was concerned. Only those items describing the emotional intensity of the experience revealed the special role played by partner sex: after having intercourse roughly twice as many men and women are "happy" as compared to after masturbating, and they also described intercourse much more often as "a passionate experience" (Figure 11).

DISCUSSION

In this paper we have looked into shifts in the significance of masturbation over the past thirty years in two steps. In the first we were able to

FIGURE 9. Attitude Towards Masturbation in Steady Relationships (1996) (%)*

	Men	Women
Reason for last masturbation		
"We couldn't have sex together"	50	40
"I just felt like it"	50	60
Attitude towards masturbation in steady relationships		
should not occur	4	5
should only be a substitute	24	19
is a form of sex in its own right	73	76

* Only students who have masturbated during current steady relationship

FIGURE 10. Description of Last Masturbation by Students With and Without Steady Relationship (1996)

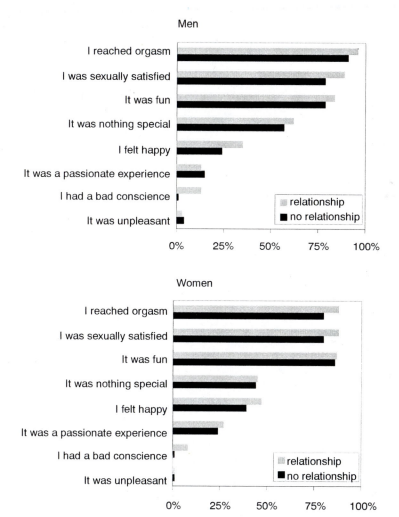

trace basic data on the incidence of masturbation over a period of thirty years and to establish that there have been marked changes during this time. In a second step we took a closer look at the way masturbation and partner sex coexisted in 1996, a phenomenon that is evidently becoming well established. Our findings extend beyond the usual basic data and

FIGURE 11. Description of Last Coitus and Last Masturbation in a Steady Relationship (1996)

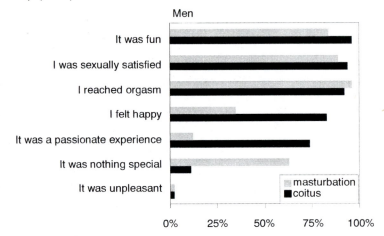

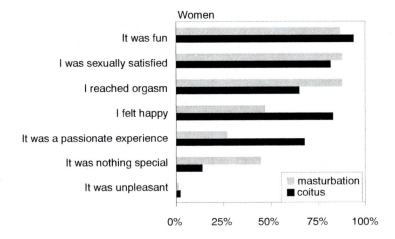

enable us to draw some tentative conclusions about the attitudes and habits associated with masturbation in steady partnerships. Our results can be summarised as follows:

1. There have been marked changes in masturbatory behaviour between 1981 and 1996. Whilst the most marked changes in

heterosexual behaviour were found between 1966 and 1981 (cf., Clement et al. 1984; Schmidt et al. 1998; Matthiesen 1999; Schmidt 2000) the shifts in masturbatory behaviour came about between 1981 and 1996. This means that the trends that Clement et al. described in 1984–masturbation at an ever earlier age and a higher incidence of it–have continued. As before, masturbation is still an area where one finds considerable differences between the genders. Nevertheless, nowadays they are becoming more alike as a result of considerable change in women's behaviour. For increasing numbers of women, one typical feature of their sexual socialisation is that they masturbate before having intercourse for the first time.

2. Masturbation has a new meaning. An examination of the data on masturbating within steady partnerships in the year 1996 brings to light signs of a new attitude: masturbation is regarded as a freely available and autonomous form of sex which no longer hovers uneasily in the wings as a stand-in, to be tolerated as a substitute if no sexual partner is available. This inference is supported amongst other things by the small differences in the responses on their masturbatory habits given by those with and those without a satisfying sexual partnership. It is also confirmed by the opinion uttered by a large number of students that masturbation is "a form of sexual activity in its own right." As such it is described in even slightly more positive terms within steady partnerships than outside them.

If we assume that the shifts between 1966 and 1981 were mainly linked to more liberal sexual attitudes that freed people of some repressions and enabled them to masturbate more freely and often, then the changes between 1981 and 1996 are above all concerned with masturbation as a form of sexual behaviour in its own right: it has lost its compensatory character and now exists for many men and women as a separate means of gaining sexual satisfaction. In this sense it is not only a relief in moments when other offers are not available, but above all an easy delight in consuming sex.

REFERENCES

Clement, Ulrich, Gunter Schmidt, & Margret Kruse: Changes in Sex Differences in Sexual Behavior: A Replication of a Study on West German Students (1966-1981). *Archives of Sexual Behavior 13*, 99-120, 1984.

Gagnon, J., & Simon, W. (1973). *Sexual Conduct. The social sources of human sexuality.* Chicago: Aldine.

Gebhard, P. H., & Johnson, A. B. (1979). *The Kinsey Data.* Bloomington, Indianapolis: Indiana University Press.

Johnson, A. M., Wadsworth, J., Wellings, K., & Field, J. (1994). *Sexual attitudes and lifestyles.* Oxford: Blackwell.

Kinsey, A. C. et al. (1948). *Sexual behavior in the human male.* Philadelphia: W.B. Saunders.

Kinsey, A. C. et al. (1953). *Sexual behavior in the human female.* Philadelphia: W.B. Saunders.

Laumann, E. O., Gagnon, J. H., Michael, R. T., & Michaels, S. (1994). *The social organization of sexuality.* Chicago, London: University Chicago Press.

Matthiesen, S. (1999). Changing gender differences in sexual behavior between the sixties and the nineties. Poster, presented at the 25th Annual Meeting of the International Academy of Sex Research, June 23-27, Stony Brook, New York.

Schmidt, G. (ed.) (2000). *Kinder der sexuellen Revolution. Kontinuität und Wandel studentischer Sexualität 1966-1996.* Giessen: Psychosozial Verlag.

Schmidt, G., & Sigusch, V. (1971). Patterns of sexual behavior in West German workers and students. *The Journal of Sex Research, 7,* 89-106.

Schmidt, G., & Sigusch, V. (1972). Changes in sexual behavior among young males and females between 1960-1970. *Archives of Sexual Behavior, 2,* 27-46.

Schmidt, G., Klusmann, D., Dekker, A., Matthiesen, S. (1998). Changes in student's sexual behaviour: 1966-1981-1996. A first report on a longitudinal study in West Germany. Scandinavian Journal of Sexology, 1, 157-173.

Spira, A., Bajos, N. & the ACSF Group (1994). *Sexual Behavior and Aids.* Aldershot, Hants: Avebury.

Masturbation in a Generational Perspective

Osmo Kontula, PhD
Elina Haavio-Mannila, PhD

ABSTRACT. Each generation has adopted views on masturbation via transforming cultural definitions of sexuality and normality. This article presents how masturbation habits have changed during the last decades in different generations and how these habits are linked to the partnership status. The analysis is based on three national follow-up sex surveys in Finland (in 1971, in 1992, and in 1999), and sex surveys in Sweden (in 1996), in Estonia (in 2000), and in St. Petersburg, Russia (in 1996).

Across these countries, each new generation had been more active in masturbation than the previous one. However, in Estonia masturbation had increased in each generation about 20 years later and in St. Petersburg about 30 years later than in Finland and Sweden. The increase in masturbation was almost unrelated to the relationship status and to the years spent in the relationship. The masturbation habits that each generation had internalized in adolescence seemed to remain unchanged through the course of their lives. The implications of these findings are that masturbation did not decrease with age and that masturbation was not a compensation for a missing sex partner but an independent way to gain sexual pleasure. The results indicate that masturbation is linked to

---

Osmo Kontula is affiliated with The Population Research Institute, The Family Federation of Finland.

Elina Haavio-Mannila is affiliated with the Department of Sociology, University of Helsinki, Finland.

Address correspondence to Osmo Kontula, The Population Research Institute, The Family Federation of Finland, P.O. Box 849, FIN-00101 Helsinki, Finland (E-mail: Osmo.Kontula@vaestoliitto.fi).

[Haworth co-indexing entry note]: "Masturbation in a Generational Perspective." Kontula, Osmo and Elina Haavio-Mannila. Co-published simultaneously in *Journal of Psychology & Human Sexuality* (The Haworth Press, Inc.) Vol. 14, No. 2/3, 2002, pp. 49-83; and: *Masturbation as a Means of Achieving Sexual Health* (ed: Walter O. Bockting and Eli Coleman) The Haworth Press, Inc., 2002, pp. 49-83. Single or multiple copies of this article are available for a fee from The Haworth Document Delivery Service [1-800-HAWORTH 9:00 a.m. - 5:00 p.m. (EST). E-mail address: getinfo@haworthpressinc.com].

the perceptions within a given culture of its nature and consequences during the teenage years of participants. *[Article copies available for a fee from The Haworth Document Delivery Service: 1-800-HAWORTH. E-mail address: <getinfo@haworthpressinc.com> Website: <http://www.HaworthPress.com> © 2002 by The Haworth Press, Inc. All rights reserved.]*

KEYWORDS. Masturbation, generations, sexual habits, sexual culture, sex history

MASTURBATION IN HISTORY

The origin of the term masturbation is in Latin "manus stuprare," that suggests self-abuse or self-defile by the hand (Kay, 1992). Some authors claim that the word more neutrally originates from the term "manus turbare" meaning to agitate or disturb by the hand. Other, more modern terms for masturbation are self-pleasuring, self-loving, self-caressing, self-fondling and self-stimulating. In this article, the traditional term masturbation will be used because of the historical and generational perspective it provides to the masturbation habits and to the feelings related to masturbation.

Historically, masturbation has been one of the most private, hidden, and underestimated sexual habits. Patton (1985) argues: "There is no other sexual behaviour so indigenous to the human species, more thoroughly discussed, more roundly condemned, yet more universally practised than masturbation." That is why the study of masturbation habits reveal issues that are essential indicators of local sexual cultures.

Even though masturbation is a private act, it has been actively regulated and negatively labeled by societies. The origins of the prejudices directed towards masturbation are in the semen conservation theory that has been very popular, for instance in Taoism. Women have been presented to compensate for their lack of semen by robbing it from men in excessive coition. In addition, it was believed that if a man ejaculates his semen inside the female genitals he lost his energy simultaneously as she gained more energy. Loss of semen in the non-reproductive activity was claimed to cause weakness and disease. A solution to this deficit was suggested to be found in semen conservation (Parrinder, 1980; Money, 1999).

In the Western sexual tradition one can speak of a masturbation panic. Some of the earliest evidence of this panic was found in the writings of Jean Gerson (1363-1429) who described masturbation as an abominable and horrid sin. His suggested remedies for masturbation included cold baths, flagellation, sobriety, prayer and good company. In the dormitories, night-lights should be kept burning, hands should be kept outside of the bedclothes, and the boys should report of their classmate's "misbehavior" (Money, 1999).

Masturbation has been an ideal target for projects of self-control that has been a part of every day moral regulation in Christianity and Judaism. Male sexual purity was declared to be a fundamental virtue in a State. It was also called a project of "civilizing an animal." With the help of sexual purity, a State could ensure sufficient healthy males fit for military service in modern mass armies (Hunt, 1998). All pleasure sensation was argued to be a satanic temptation in disguise. Because sex was the most stimulating activity of all, it was considered the most dangerous. If it was immoral, it (including masturbation) had to be unhealthy as well (Whorton, 2001).

Both religious and medical arguments have been used as weapons against masturbation. In the 18th century, there were claims that masturbation provokes mental illness as a prelude to the eternal punishment. In the texts of Simon André Tissot (1974), first published in 1758, masturbation was fully medicalized. Tissot paid special attention to the effects of masturbation on the nervous system (Stolberg, 2000). He claimed that masturbation caused an excessive blood flow to the brain that can result in impotence and insanity (Kay, 1992).

John Harvey Kellogg's (1974, originally 1877, 329-338) method of "treatment" for chronic masturbation was to set up the foreskin with silver wire, that caused enough pain to prevent masturbation, and to burn off the clitoris with carbolic acid (Money, 1999; Money, 1985). Any kinds of means were justified in the war against masturbation. Originally, male circumcision was started with the hope that it could prevent male masturbation. Later this origin was gradually forgotten and revised arguments were presented to legitimate the male circumcision.

The Western medical profession created the concept of post-masturbatory disease that could cause impotence (Stolberg, 2000). Masturbating women were said to develop an unnaturally enlarged, penis-like clitoris, or to lose their attractiveness. According to the masturbation neurosis hypothesis, excessive masturbation was claimed to cause draining of sexual energy that could give rise to neurasthenia or neurosis (Kay, 1992). And still, physical damage caused by masturbation was argued to make a person engaged in masturbation incapable of consummating the marriage or of having children (Stolberg, 2000). The aim of these invented threats was to prevent masturbation via fear and guilt. In sum, masturbation-guilt has been also the centrepiece of erotophobia (Tiefer, 1998).

Masturbation anxiety has been shown to be at its peak in the early 1900s (Hall, 1992). The generation which lived its childhood in the early 1900s was the most afraid of the possible health damages caused by masturbation acts. Some of the practical implications of this "sex education" were found in the several thousands of letters sent to the scientist Marie Stolpes (the author of several sex manuals) in 1918-1945 (Hall, 1992). These letters reveal many sorts of anxieties over masturbation. Some writers could name the literal source that caused their anxiety:

> Somehow I got hold at the age of nineteen of a book called 'What a Young Man Ought to Know.' Having read it, and with a violent assertion of willpower, I overcame the vice of masturbation, and have kept free from it ever since.

> When I was about twenty-two, I had a nervous breakdown. It was not until I read that book that I realised what harm I had been doing to my health through a self-abuse.

Some doctors considered prostitutes to be better for their patients than masturbation:

> I was told and I believed, that the only possible alternative to this (masturbation) was to go with prostitutes, and that this alternative was more degrading than the other.

> The doctor strongly advised me to drop masturbation. He even suggested certain houses where I might meet women of a better class, and advised the use of sheaths or injections. The doctor even advised women as a lesser evil than the risk of disease in masturbation.

Some people were trying to rid themselves of masturbation by increasing the frequency of their intercourse:

> Before I was married, I used to have unions three and four times a night, two or three times a week with different girls in the hope of curing myself but it was of no use.

A true man was presented to be able to control his sexual urges.

"Studies in the Psychology of Sex" by Havelock Ellis (1910, originally 1899) was the first book to attempt to break off some prejudices toward masturbation. According to Ellis, only habitual, prolonged masturbation could be harmful. In the U.S., in the 1920s and 1930s, the more sophisticated members of the medical community launched a full-scale assault on the myths of masturbatory insanity, but it took another generation before the myths were exposed to the general public (Bullough, 1987).

These myths related to masturbation were at last challenged in the West in the sexual revolution that was launched in the 1960s. New sources of information were available and sexual issues and values related to sexuality were reassessed. Sexual science blossomed. Masturbation was not only approved, it was also recommend to be used as an important technique in the exercises of sex therapy (Kaplan, 1975). Instead of being a dangerous sin, masturbation was defined to be a virtue by which individuals could promote their well-being and skills for sexual interaction. This was assumed to have an impact on the masturbation habits especially among the better educated who had the new knowledge at their disposal.

This article attempts to show how masturbation habits have changed during the last decades in different generations in two Nordic countries and in two parts of the former Soviet Union. With the help of sex surveys we present how masturbation has been related to different relationship statuses and how masturbation activities can be explained by social background and people's sexual ideas and activities.

Nordic countries have been pioneers in the Western sexual revolution with it's public debates and wide distribution of sex education, information, pornography and literature about sex (Kontula & Kosonen, 1996). This has been assumed to have decreased the fears and guilt associated with masturbation habits in Western countries.

In the Soviet Union (after a short period of sexual liberalization following the 1917 revolution), the sexual policy enforced heterosexual monogamous family life and motherhood (Liljeström, 1995). Up until the 1980s, sexual education and research on sexuality had to be very limited in scope, while small amounts of information and moral advice featured in medical and pedagogical journals. All other public discussion of so called intimate questions were censored.

Still in 1990s there were several authorities who described masturbation as psychologically harmful and a cause of excessive morbidity and mortality (Kon, 1995, 199, 267; Rotkirch, 2000, 173). Similar warnings were presented still in the early 1990s in the Estonian medical school (Poolamets, 2001). This is assumed to have inhibited masturbation in many parts of the former Soviet Union, even in the young cohorts, much more than in the Western countries where more reasonable sex education has been available since the 1960s.

METHOD

The data for this article was gathered by six sex surveys conducted toward the end of the 20th century in two Nordic and two former Soviet areas. The main data is from Finland, where three national population sexuality surveys have been conducted. First, there was the 1971 survey of 2,188 participants (age-group 18-54) with face-to-face interviews in which each interviewee also completed a self-administered questionnaire. The response rate was 91%. Second, in the 1992 survey, the data collection method was identical and the number of respondents was 2,250 (age-group 18-74). The response rate was 76%. Third, in 1999 a similar mail survey was conducted with 1,556 responses (age-group 18-81), with a response rate of 46%. In order to correct for a bias in the demographic composition of the data, it was weighted by age and gender. As a result, the demographic structure of the data now represents that of the original sample.

According to some characteristics other than age and gender, the 1999 data don't seem to be biased. By analyzing the distributions of several identical retrospective questions measuring sexual issues in different generations, Kontula (2001) could show that the low response rate in 1999 has not had any major impact on the results of sex history among those who were less than 55 years old. In the age group 55-74 the male respondents were more monogamous than on the average in that age group.

In their analyses of the Western sex surveys, Michaels and Giami (1999) wrote about the Finnish (1992) sex survey: "The Finnish survey appears as a turning point, a kind of hybrid between the 1970's model of sex surveys and the subsequent 1990's AIDS-related sex surveys. It reflects the long-term trend toward 'sexual optimism' increasingly considering sex as a positive and fulfilling experience that has characterized modern sex research from Havelock Ellis to Masters and Johnson."

In the same period when the later Finnish surveys were carried out, comparable national sex surveys were conducted in Sweden (1996), Estonia (2000) and St. Petersburg (1996). The results of these surveys will in some cases be compared with those of the three follow-up surveys in Finland. In Sweden and St. Petersburg, the data collection took place in a similar manner as in Finland in 1971 and 1992. In Sweden, a representative sample was drawn from the central population register of the state (Lewin et al., 1998). In St. Petersburg, the voting register was used as the sampling base (Gronow et al., 1997). In Sweden and St. Petersburg, the respondents answered to the general questions orally, face-to-face and then completed the intimate part of the questionnaire by themselves in paper-and-pencil. The response rate was 59% in Sweden and 60% in St. Petersburg. The respondents were representative of the general population in regard to gender and age (Lewin et al., 1998; Haavio-Mannila & Rotkirch, 1998; Haavio-Mannila & Kontula, 2001).

In Estonia, the universes of the Omnibus type surveys, carried out by the market research organization Emor twice a month, are comprised of the permanent residents of the Republic of Estonia at the age of 15-74, 1.1 million people, as of January 1st, 1999. Each time the sample size was 500 persons. The sex survey was repeated five times in May-August 2000. The data collection took place in the following way: The interviewers took the questionnaires to the respondents, who completed and returned them to Emor. Of the selected persons 1,031 (41%) returned the questionnaire.

Emor formed the samples by two-staged stratified sampling method. First, the universe is divided by territorial domicile into six strata. Then, a two stages selection is done in each stratum. The primary sampling units are settlements. In each primary sampling unit the secondary sampling units–individuals–are chosen. Eight persons are interviewed at each sampling point. In towns, addresses are selected at random from the population register. After the apartment or private house is chosen by means of random route method, the youngest male at home, and if not present, the youngest female aged 15-74 is interviewed. In rural areas, the addresses are selected at random from the list of residents provided by the local parish administrations. Also here, the so-called young-men-rule is used for selecting individuals in selected households.

To check the sample, its socio-demographic structure is compared to the corresponding data of the universe. The data are weighted to ensure the representativeness of the sample. Among our respondents, there were more people living in the capital, Tallinn, and in rural areas than in the other towns and cities; the proportion of men was lower; there were more 25- to 34-year-olds and less 55- to 74-year olds, and more national

Estonians than in the population at large. In order to correct for these biases, the data was weighted by type of settlement, gender, age, and nationality.

The frequency of masturbation was measured in the Finnish, Estonian and St. Petersburg surveys by using a question with the exact same wording (see Table 2). It covers both lifetime and current masturbation activities. In Sweden masturbation habits were studied, for instance, by asking "How old were you when you masturbated (satisfied yourself) for the first time?" "How many times have you masturbated during the last 30 days?" On the basis of these two questions we can compare the Swedish data on lifetime and monthly masturbation with the data from the other areas. In addition to studying masturbation habits, in the Finnish samples, people's perceptions of health hazards of masturbation were also examined.

The generations were analyzed in 13 birth cohorts. The cohorts were born in 1917-1921, 1922-1926, 1927-1931, 1932-1936, 1937-1941, 1942-1946, 1947-1951, 1952-1956, 1957-1961, 1962-1966, 1967-1971, 1972-1976 and 1977-1980. In addition to presenting distributions and means according to age, gender and area, the data has been analyzed by using Multiple Classification Analysis (MCA), a type of regression analysis, in which the dependent variable has to be an interval scale but the independent variables can be non-parametric, that is, ordinal scales or categorical response alternatives.

RESULTS

Opinions on the Healthiness of Masturbation

The warnings presented against masturbation in the textbooks and in the media have had an impact on the individual cognition and feelings related to masturbation. This can be seen in the Finnish sex surveys in 1992 and 1999 where responses to the statement "Masturbation does not endanger health" were studied. Respondents could entirely or somewhat agree or disagree with the statement or respond "hard to say."

The proportion of respondents entirely agreeing with the statement was 52% for both genders in 1992 and for men 63% and women 59% in 1999. These persons were not at all worried about the unhealthiness of masturbation. Roughly one-third of the respondents born before 1940 agreed entirely with the statement (Figure 1). Among the respondents who were born after the beginning of the 1950s, the proportion was

FIGURE 1. Agrees Entirely with the Statement, "Masturbation Doesn't Endanger Health," by Generations in the 1990s in Finland

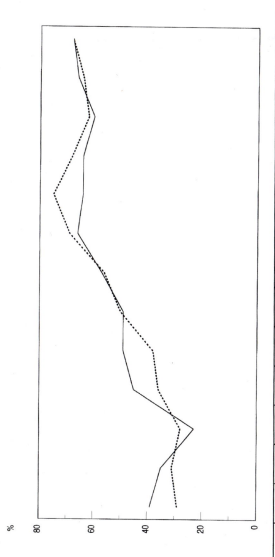

Year of birth	1917-1921	1922-1926	1927-1931	1932-1936	1937-1941	1942-1946	1947-1951	1952-1956	1957-1961	1962-1966	1967-1971	1972-1976	1977-1980
Men —	39	35	23	45	49	49	57	66	64	64	60	66	68
Women ...	29	31	28	36	38	50	56	69	75	68	62	64	58

much higher: about two-thirds. The ideas concerning the healthiness of masturbation had "revolutionarily" changed for men who were teenagers in the 1950s. For teenage women, the change toward not being worried about the health hazards of masturbation happened in the beginning of the 1960s. A second turning-point for men was in the late 1960s and for women in the early 1970s. On the average, men had adopted more positive ideas about masturbation 5-10 years earlier than women. However, for people who were adolescents since the 1970s, the ideas about masturbation have remained fairly similar.

Uncertainty of the health effects of masturbation was related to a lack of other kind of relevant information and education. This can be seen by looking at the attitudes toward masturbation according to the length of education of the respondents (Table 1). The Finns with fewer years of education were most often uncertain of the unhealthiness of masturbation. The proportions of uncertain respondents were two to five times higher among those who had a low level of education as opposed to those with higher education who were more likely to be certain that masturbation was not unhealthy. This was true for both genders and both surveys in Finland in the 1990s.

Still in 1999, one fourth of the Finnish respondents in the younger generation (18-34 years of age) were not absolutely sure if masturbation was healthy or not (Haavio-Mannila, Kontula & Kuusi, 2001, 121-122). The fears and guilt related to masturbation were evident even though some decrease in the ignorance was found. According to the U.S. sex survey (Laumann et al., 1994), every second man and woman reported feeling guilty after masturbation. These feelings existed quite similarly in different age groups. Even the younger generations had not succeeded to get rid of fears and guilt related to masturbation.

MASTURBATION HABITS IN DIFFERENT COUNTRIES

Anxiety about masturbation has had a major impact on the actual behavior. A high proportion of participants abstained from masturbation for their entire life. The difference between Finland/Sweden and the former Soviet Union is great (Table 2). The distributions of recency of masturbation in Estonia in 2000 resemble those in Finland in 1971. In St. Petersburg in 1996, masturbation was even more rare than in Finland in 1971. Most St. Petersburg women had never masturbated. The women born before the second world war in St. Petersburg abstained from masturbation almost completely (Figure 2). Even in the young

TABLE 1. Reactions to statement "masturbation does not endanger health" (range 1-5, high scores indicate agreement), according to gender and years in education in Finland in 1992 and 1999, unadjusted and age-adjusted means. Multiple classification analysis.

Gender and Years in Education	N	Predicted mean, unadjusted	Predicted mean, adjusted	Eta	Beta, adjusted for factors	P <	R Squared
Men							
Finland 1992							
-8	282	3.95	4.03				
9-10	202	4.15	4.15				
11-13	356	4.24	4.20				
14-	259	4.47	4.44	.190	.152	.001	.041
Finland 1999							
-8	133	4.09	4.24				
9-10	113	4.08	4.13				
11-13	200	4.48	4.40				
14-	224	4.63	4.58	.241	.171	.001	.082
Women							
Finland 1992							
-8	315	3.78	3.94				
9-10	238	4.05	4.08				
11-13	310	4.27	4.17				
14-	276	4.57	4.49	.294	.204	.001	.102
Finland 1999							
-8	128	3.92	1.13				
9-10	109	4.00	4.10				
11-13	206	4.35	4.25				
14-	248	4.59	4.52	.262	.173	.001	.101

generation only half of the women in St. Petersburg had masturbated in their life time.

In the generations born before the 1930s, most women in Finland, Sweden and Estonia had abstained from masturbation. In Estonia, until those born in the 1960s, half of the women avoided masturbation. In the youngest Estonian generations, the proportions of women not reporting masturbation were still about one third. Looking at the trends in the different generations, it seems that the increase in female masturbation had taken place in St. Petersburg 40 years and in Estonia 30 years later than in Finland and Sweden. We assume that this difference is to a great extent due to the more negative information available about masturbation in the former Soviet Union than in the Nordic countries.

Comparing Finland and Sweden, the proportions of women inexperienced in masturbation were fairly similar in each generation. In the younger generations only about 10% of women had abstained from

TABLE 2. Replies to the question: "when was the last time when you practised masturbation?" by 18-to-54 year-old men and women in Sweden, Finland, Estonia and St. Petersburg, %.

Gender/Time Since Last Masturbation Event	Sweden 1996	Finland 1971	Finland 1992	Finland 1992	Estonia 2000	St. Petersburg 1996
Men						
Never	3	26	10	6	31	35
More than 10 years ago	..	16	13	8	9	23
1-10 years ago	30 [1]	16	16	12	10	15
During the past year	..	14	20	14	12	9
During the past month	29	14	19	21	12	10
During the past week	36	11	20	27	15	6
During the past 24 hours	2	3	4	12	11	2
Total	100	100	100	100	100	100
N	1,089	1,037	845	513	284	588
Women						
Never	15	49	23	14	45	68
More than 10 years ago	..	9	16	8	2	7
1-10 years ago	43	14	16	16	6	6
During the past year	..	12	21	25	18	8
During the past month	30	9	14	20	14	6
During the past week	11	6	9	13	10	4
During the past 24 hours	1	1	1	4	5	1
Total	100	100	100	100	100	100
N	974	990	611	501	468	808

1) Has not masturbated during the last month but has done it during lifetime.

masturbation. In these countries, the turning point for women seems to have been in the generation that were teenagers in the early 1960s and later. This is consistent with the results on the change of ideas related to the healthiness of masturbation that took place at the same time. The misinformation on the health hazards of masturbation apparently had a strong impact on masturbation habits in the generations of women who were teenagers before 1960s.

For men, the proportions inexperienced in masturbation were lower than those of women (Figure 3). In St. Petersburg and Estonia about one-half of men born before the 1950s had never masturbated. In the young generations, still 20-30% of the Estonian and St. Petersburg men had never masturbated. There was a fairly steady decline in the rates of

FIGURE 2. Women in Finland, Sweden, Estonia and St. Petersburg Who Have Never Masturbated

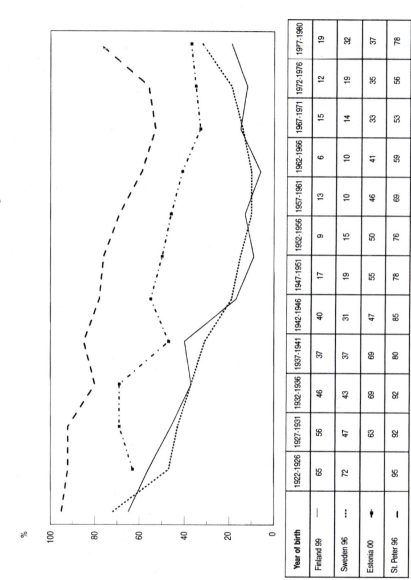

Year of birth		1922-1926	1927-1931	1932-1936	1937-1941	1942-1946	1947-1951	1952-1956	1957-1961	1962-1966	1967-1971	1972-1976	1977-1980
Finland 99	—	65	56	46	37	40	17	9	13	6	15	12	19
Sweden 96	...	72	47	43	37	31	19	15	10	10	14	19	32
Estonia 00	–·–		63	69	69	47	55	50	46	41	33	35	37
St. Peter 96	–	95	92	92	80	85	78	76	69	59	53	56	78

FIGURE 3. Men in Finland, Sweden, Estonia and St. Petersburg Who Have Never Masturbated

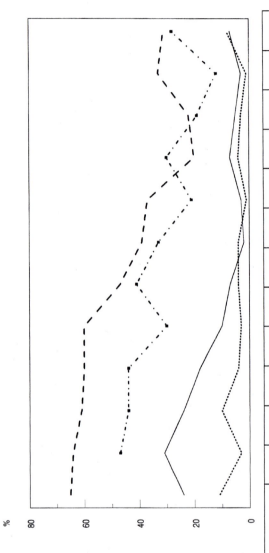

%

Year of Birth		1922-1926	1927-1931	1932-1936	1937-1941	1942-1946	1947-1951	1952-1956	1957-1961	1962-1966	1967-1971	1972-1976	1977-1980
Finland 99	—	24	31	24	18	10	7	2	3	7	5	3	7
Sweden 96	····	11	3	10	4	3	4	4	1	4	3	1	8
Estonia 00	–·–		47	44	44	30	41	33	21	30	19	12	28
St. Peter 96	—	65	64	61	60	60	47	39	37	20	22	33	31

62

people without experiences of masturbation. This decline started among men who were teenagers after the beginning of the 1960s. The Western sexual revolution seems to have had some impact on sexual habits also in the former Soviet Union but the timing of the trends differs significantly from that in the Nordic countries (Kon, 1995; Rotkirch, 2000). The Gorbachev policy of glasnost eventually led to the liberalization of the printed word and a Russian public "sexual revolution" in 1989, when topics such as abortions, birth clinics, contraceptives, and young people's sexuality entered into public debate (Kon, 1995, 267).

In Finland, a quarter of the men born before the 1940s had never masturbated. In this age group men were more active in masturbation in Sweden than in Finland. In the younger generations, only a few percent of men had never masturbated. The younger Nordic men were not afraid of experimenting with masturbation.

A look at the current masturbation habits (i.e., masturbation during the last month) reveals that the younger generations have been much more active masturbators than the older generations (Figures 4 and 5). Among the older people, 20-30% of men and a few percent of women had masturbated during the last month. In St. Petersburg, the oldest men had masturbated as seldom as women in Estonia and Finland. Of the youngest men, about 80% in Finland and Sweden, one-half in Estonia, but only one-quarter in St. Petersburg had masturbated during the last month. Among women, the respective proportions of masturbators were about one-half in Finland and Sweden, one-third in Estonia, and one-fifth in St. Petersburg.

In Sweden both men and women of all generations had masturbated somewhat more often than men and women in Finland. Estonians had masturbated less than Finns but more than people in St. Petersburg. Estonian women resembled Finnish women more than Estonian men resembled Finnish men. On the average, in all the areas studied, the rate of monthly masturbation of women was almost 40 percent units lower than that of men.

Masturbation activities stayed very stable in Finland across time for each generation or birth cohort. For instance, the proportion of people who had masturbated during the last month was almost identical in every birth cohort and among both genders according to all three sex surveys, in spite of the fact that the respondents of the last survey were on the average 27 years older than those in the first survey (Figures 6 and 7). The masturbation habits that every generation adopted during its teenage years seemed to have remained unchanged throughout people's

FIGURE 4. Masturbation by Women During the Last Month in Finland, Sweden, Estonia and St. Petersburg

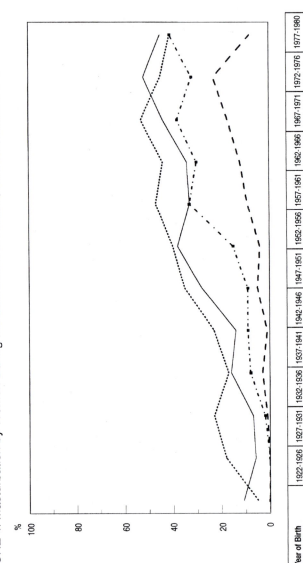

Year of Birth		1922-1926	1927-1931	1932-1936	1937-1941	1942-1946	1947-1951	1952-1956	1957-1961	1962-1966	1967-1971	1972-1976	1977-1980
Finland	—	11	6	7	16	14	28	38	33	34	44	52	45
Sweden	···	5	18	23	17	23	35	40	47	44	53	45	41
Estonia	┆	0	0	2	8	9	9	15	33	30	38	32	41
St. Peters	–	0	0	1	3	1	5	4	9	12	17	23	8

FIGURE 5. Masturbation by Men During the Last Month in Finland, Sweden, Estonia and St. Petersburg

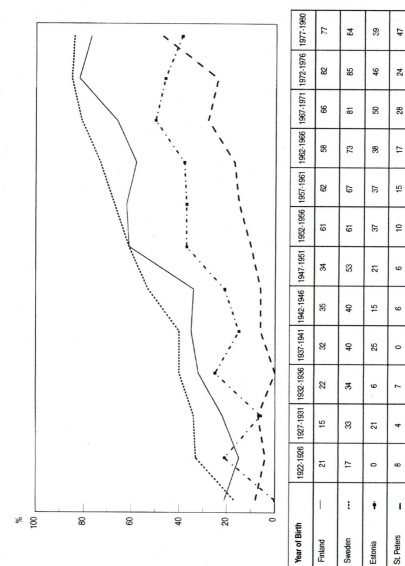

Year of Birth		1922-1926	1927-1931	1932-1936	1937-1941	1942-1946	1947-1951	1952-1956	1957-1961	1962-1966	1967-1971	1972-1976	1977-1990
Finland	—	21	15	22	32	35	34	61	62	58	66	82	77
Sweden	...	17	33	34	40	40	53	61	67	73	81	85	84
Estonia	▪	0	21	6	25	15	21	37	37	38	50	46	39
St. Peters	—	8	4	7	0	6	6	10	15	17	28	24	47

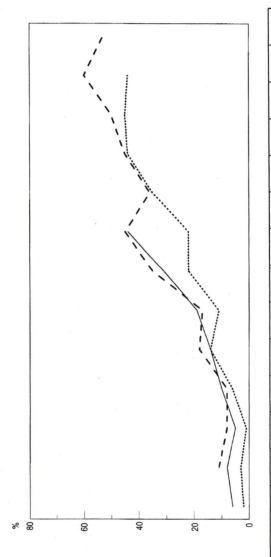

FIGURE 6. Women Who Masturbated During the Last Month by Generation in Three Sex Surveys in Finland

Year of Birth	1917-1921	1922-1926	1927-1931	1932-1936	1937-1941	1942-1946	1947-1951	1952-1956	1957-1961	1962-1966	1967-1971	1972-1976	1977-1980
Finland 71 —	6	8	5	10	14	19	31	44					
Finland 92 ...	2	3	1	6	14	11	22	22	35	44	45	44	
Finland 99 —		11	8	8	18	17	35	45	36	45	50	60	53

FIGURE 7. Men Who Masturbated During the Last Month by Generation in Three Sex Surveys in Finland

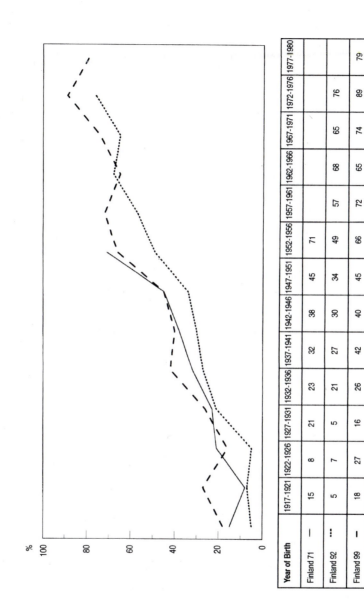

Year of Birth		1917-1921	1922-1926	1927-1931	1932-1936	1937-1941	1942-1946	1947-1951	1952-1956	1957-1961	1962-1966	1967-1971	1972-1976	1977-1980
Finland 71	—	15	8	21	23	32	38	45	71					
Finland 92	····	5	7	5	21	27	30	34	49	57	68	65	76	
Finland 99	—	18	27	16	26	42	40	45	66	72	65	74	89	79

life course. People who were not interested in masturbation when they were young, were also not interested in masturbation throughout the rest of their life. This means that aging in and of itself does not seem to have much of an effect on the practice of masturbation. Instead of the biological age, the quality of sex education and public opinion about masturbation in society during the teenage period of each generation seems to be of utmost importance for the future masturbation habits of each generation.

These results can be compared to some other findings from the Western sex surveys. Unfortunately, in the sex surveys of the late 1980s and early 1990s, masturbation was seldom measured (Michaels & Giami, 1999). Of several other European surveys, it was studied only in France (Spira et al., 1994) and in The Netherlands (Sandfort et al., 1998). Comparisons to these surveys are difficult because the questions did not measure masturbation over lifetime (as here), but only at the time of the survey.

Comparisons with the French and the Dutch studies show that gender differences in masturbation activities were in the 1990s much larger in France and the Netherlands than in Finland and Sweden. In France there were more women who never masturbated. Another finding is that in France and the Netherlands, the younger generation of women was not much more active in masturbation than the older generations of women. There was no similar increase in the masturbation rates from one generation to the other as we found in Northern Europe.

According to the findings by Laumann et al. (1994), masturbation has been less common in the United States than in Finland. For men less than 60 years of age, 37% in the U.S. compared to 28% in Finland had not masturbated at all during the last month. For women, these proportions were 58% and 39%, respectively. This means that masturbation was much more common in Finland than in the U.S. This holds true in all age groups under the age of 60. The most visible difference between the U.S. and Finland was in the young generation, among the 18- to 24-year-olds (Laumann et al., 1994, 81-82; Haavio-Mannila & Kontula, 2001, 244-245). The increase in the practice of masturbation from the older to the younger generations was much more remarkable in Finland, Sweden, Estonia and St. Petersburg than in the United States.

Twenty-seven percent of U.S. men compared to 37% of Finnish men reported masturbating during the last week. For women these proportions were 8% and 17%, respectively. In the generation less than 40 years of age, women in Finland reported masturbating twice as often as women in the U.S during the last week.

In the developing world, masturbation has been an even stronger taboo than in those countries studied here. In India only a third of the college women ever masturbated. All of them had strong feelings of anxiety and guilt (Sharma & Sharma, 1998). In Turkey parents have even looked for medical help for their daughters, but not for their sons, in the case of masturbation (Unal, 2000).

MASTURBATION IN DIFFERENT TYPES OF RELATIONSHIPS

In the U.S., cohabiting individuals have been characterized by comparatively high rates of masturbation (Laumann et al., 1994). Is this true also in Finland where we can look at this issue over time?

In Finland in the 1990s, masturbation was most common among men who were single at the time of the survey. In 1999, two-thirds of single men had reported masturbating during the last month. The men who were "living apart/together," i.e., lived separately from their permanent partner, ranked second in terms of masturbation during the last month, and the cohabiting men third. The married men reported masturbating least often. Part of these differences can be contributed to the different average age of the people with different relationship status.

Masturbation had increased in the 1990s in each of these relationship types, most visibly among those who were married (Figure 8). For women, differences between the cohabiting, living apart together, and single women were small.

Almost 40% of the women belonging to the three non-married relationship status groups had masturbated during the last month. When the influence of age was controlled for, the proportion of those who reported masturbating in the last month of the cohabiting and living apart together people declined to about 30%, whereas the masturbation rate of single women remained the same (39%). Older cohabiting and separately-living women resembled married women who masturbated least often of all gender and relationship type groups. This was partly due to their higher average age; controlling for age increased the proportion of people who reported masturbating in the last month among married women from 21% to 25%.

Married men masturbated twice as often as married women. However, the married women had almost doubled their masturbation in the 1990s, from 13% to 21%. More and more men and women seem to continue masturbation after getting married.

FIGURE 8. Masturbation During the Last Month in Different Types of Relationships in Finland in 1992 and 1999

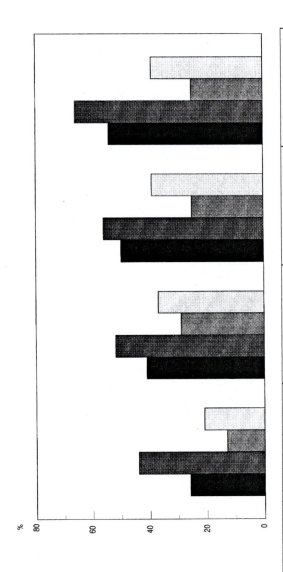

Relationship	Marriage	Cohabitation	Go Steady	Single
Men 92	26	41	50	54
Men 99	44	52	56	66
Women 92	13	29	25	25
Women 99	21	37	39	39

This can be seen more clearly by looking at the masturbation rates according to the number of years the respondents had stayed in their present relationship (from 1-40+ years) in the three Finnish surveys (Figures 9 and 10). In 1992 and 1999, the data includes the married, those who cohabited and those who lived apart/together; the relationships that had lasted more than ten years were almost always marriages. In 1971, the results apply only to married respondents.

Having masturbated increased in each relationship category from one survey to the next (in time). Masturbation also increased in relationships that had lasted a long time. Some people still have an interest in masturbation after a relationship of 40 years, which was almost always marriage. This supports our earlier conclusion that marriage does not necessarily inhibit masturbation activities. With time, men in a sexual relationship increased their masturbation more than women in a sexual relationship. The largest growth had taken place among women who had just started their relationship. They had tripled their masturbation from 1971 to 1999. Among men, masturbation quintupled among those who had been married between 10-19 years.

PREDICTORS OF RECENT MASTURBATION

Masturbation increased from one generation to another among both the respondents with a steady sexual partner and those who were single. During the same time, there was a growing number of Finns who considered masturbation as a healthy habit. Which social and cultural factors promoted this change?

One of the promoters of this change is education. Finns with more education expressed less unjustified fears and guilt about masturbation than those with less education. The more educated seldom considered masturbation unhealthy (Table 1 above).

As described above, education also seemed to have an impact on those who are uncertain about the effects of masturbation on health. The proportion of respondents who were uncertain of the healthiness of masturbation was lower among those with more education.

With regards to behavior, the more educated masturbated more often during the last month than the less educated (Table 3). This was true in Finland as well as in Estonia. In Sweden it held true to some extent. The lowest educated women masturbated less than those with middle and high levels of education. However, in St. Petersburg, education was not

FIGURE 9. Women Who Have Masturbated During the Last Month by Years in Present Relationship in Three Sex Surveys in Finland

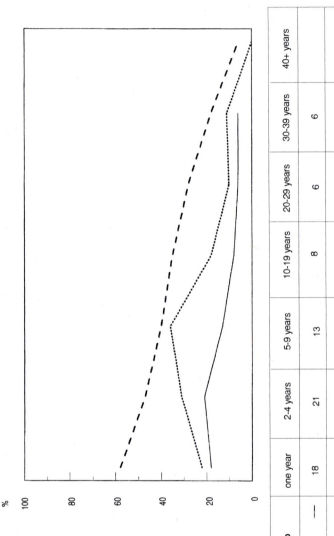

Relationship		one year	2-4 years	5-9 years	10-19 years	20-29 years	30-39 years	40+ years
Finland 71	—	18	21	13	8	6	6	0
Finland 92	.....	22	31	36	18	10	11	0
Finland 99	- -	58	47	40	35	28	18	6

FIGURE 10. Men Who Have Masturbated During the Last Month by Years in Present Relationship in Three Sex Surveys in Finland

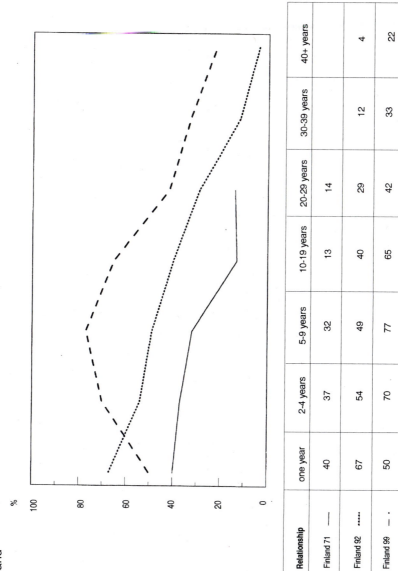

Relationship	one year	2-4 years	5-9 years	10-19 years	20-29 years	30-39 years	40+ years
Finland 71 ——	40	37	32	13	14		
Finland 92 ·····	67	54	49	40	29	12	4
Finland 99 —·—	50	70	77	65	42	33	22

TABLE 3. Education and age as predictors of monthly masturbation of men and women in Sweden, Finland, Estonia and St. Petersburg. Unadjusted and age-adjusted percentages. Multiple classification analysis.

Gender/Area/Education	N	Predicted mean, unadjusted	Predicted mean, age adjusted	Eta	Beta, adjusted for age	P <	R Squared
Men							
Sweden 1996							
Academic	329	59	65				
College	388	66	61				
Vocational school	410	59	59				
None	187	59	58	.066	.055	.202	.163
Finland 1992							
Academic	87	40	40				
College	142	48	46				
Vocational school	392	36	33				
None	405	31	34	.119	.087	.028	.148
Finland 1999							
Academic	73	56	58				
College	147	62	60				
Vocational school	235	47	42				
None	199	46	52	.128	.148	.001	.170
Estonia							
Academic	731	34	36				
College	642	36	35				
Vocational school or less	212	24	25	0.1	0.115	0	0.061
St. Petersburg							
Academic	298	11	14				
College	235	16	13				
Vocational school or less	333	12	11	0	0.045	0.4	0.062
Women							
Sweden 1996							
Academic	287	37	34				
College	282	40	40				
Vocational school	241	42	41				
None	349	30	34	0.1	0.068	.129	.063
Finland 1992							
Academic	72	35	33				
College	194	24	20				
Vocational school	326	13	12				
None	476	19	22	.146	.145	.001	.116
Finland 1999							
Academic	93	52	50				
College	179	25	24				
Vocational school	172	29	28				
None	213	24	26	.202	.186	.001	.124
Estonia							
Academic	123	26	28				
College	231	22	20				
Vocational school or less	187	17	17	0	0.093	0	0.099
St. Petersburg							
Academic	392	8	9				
College	394	9	8				
Vocational school or less	421	6	6	0	0.045	0.3	0.057

TABLE 4. Predictors of recent masturbation in Finland in 1992 and 1999 (combined), unadjusted and age-adjusted means (range 1-71). Multiple classification analysis.

Predictor	N	Predicted mean, unadjusted	Predicted mean, adjusted	Eta	Beta, adjusted for factors and covariates	P <
"Masturbation does not endanger health"						
Absolutely agree	1,844	4.10	3.91			
Somewhat agree	615	3.22	3.34			
Difficult to say	597	2.10	2.48			
Disagree slightly	61	2.46	2.78			
Absolutely disagree	64	2.64	2.95	.436	.310	.001
Age at first intercourse						
-15	452	3.89	3.46			
16-17	938	3.70	3.48			
18-19	914	3.46	3.51			
20-21	438	3.17	3.42			
22-	440	3.03	3.57	.156	.024	.591
Intercourse during last month						
Not at all	604	3.38	3.77			
Once	272	3.64	3.81			
Once or twice	628	3.48	3.59			
Once a week	610	3.40	3.44			
At least twice a week	1,068	3.58	3.23	.051	.123	.001
Watched sex videos last year						
No or no information	1,975	3.00	3.29			
Yes	1,207	4.30	3.82	.347	.143	.001
Sexual partners during last year						
No or no information	323	2.96	3.60			
1	2,251	3.32	3.40			
2	275	4.31	3.82			
3	136	4.55	3.75			
4	66	4.35	3.74			
5+	130	4.56	3.73	.258	.084	.001
Years of education						
-8	698	2.44	3.13			
9-10	577	3.14	3.37			
11-13	965	3.78	3.46			
14+	942	4.19	3.86	.363	.147	.001
Intoxication						
Never	1,117	2.65	3.25			
Yearly	1,094	3.63	3.53			
Monthly	791	4.19	3.65			
Weekly	180	4.75	3.99	.376	.112	.001
Place of living						
Helsinki	320	3.99	3.65			
Other city of over 100,000 inhabitants	565	3.74	3.59			
A city or town of 20,000-100,000 inhabitants	824	3.58	3.50			
A city or town of under 20,000 inhabitants	373	3.39	3.44			
Rural centre	656	3.39	3.45	.165	.048	.041
Elsewhere in a rural area	445	2.90	3.35			

1) The scale values are: 1 never, 2 more than 10 years ago, 3 1-10 years ago, 4 during the last year, 5 during the last month, 6 during the last week, and 7 during the last 24 hours.

The statistical significance of all covariates, age, gender, and single status, p < .001.
Variance explained (R squared) .418.

at all related to people's masturbation habits. In Russia, masturbation seemed to be a taboo topic across educational groups.

A similar relationship between masturbation and education has been found in the U.S. (Laumann et al., 1994). Eighty percent of men who had graduate degrees reported masturbating in the past year, and this proportion declined in a stair-step fashion to 45% of those who had not completed high school. A similar pattern was found among women. Sixty percent of women who attended graduate school reported masturbating in the past year. The proportion of masturbators declined to 25% among those women who did not complete high school.

Other European surveys have found that people with a stronger sexual desire masturbate more. Those who report an earlier age of first intercourse, more sexual partners, with more frequent intercourse, and more liberal sexual attitudes, usually report masturbating more (Sandfort et al., 1998.) In the U.S., the most important motivation for masturbation was found to be relieving sexual tension and obtaining physical pleasure (Laumann et al., 1994).

We assumed that sexual motivation and desire for sexual pleasure would be important predictors of active masturbation. There are many indicators of sexual desire, such as the frequency of intercourse, the number of sexual partners, age of first intercourse, and use of pornography. Masturbation was also hypothesized to be common among people who are not afraid of the health hazards of masturbation, who were actively looking for other types of pleasure (e.g., intoxication with alcohol), and among people living in urban areas where sexual scripts are more permissive than in the countryside. Because age, type of relationship, and education were already found to be important demographic predictors of masturbation, they were included in the Multiple Classification Analysis as covariates in order to predict recent masturbation in Finland (Table 4; the classification of recency of masturbation is presented in the footnote of the table).

In Finland, recent masturbation was in the 1990s strongly related to frequent intercourse in the last month, number of partners in the last month, watching of sexually-explicit videos during the last year, and lack of fear of health hazards of masturbation. In addition, respondents who often got drunk, had higher education, and lived in an urban area, masturbated more than those who were sober, lower educated, and rural. Being male, young, and single were other characteristics associated with frequent masturbation.

The association between age at first intercourse and recent masturbation was weak among men, and its significance disappeared when other factors were controlled for. Among women, however, the association between age at first intercourse and masturbation was very strong. Of the women who started coitus before the age of 16, 31% in 1992 and 40% in 1999 reported masturbating in a month whereas the proportions for the late starters (22+ years) were only 9% and 13%, respectively. The gender difference in masturbation was very small among early starters compared to the late starters of intercourse.

The increase in masturbation rate in different categories according to the time of last intercourse, number of sexual partners, and use of pornographic materials was also examined in Finland. Masturbation increased between 1971 and 1999 almost without any relationship to the frequency of intercourse (Kontula, 2001b). This means that those with a high frequency of intercourse had increased masturbation as much as those who had had intercourse less frequently. Furthermore, masturbation increased during the same time span as much among those with no or one partner as among those with several partners in a year. Between 1992 and 1999 (there is no corresponding data from 1971), masturbation increased regardless of whether or not one used pornography. These three results indicate that the growth in masturbation has taken place at the same pace among people with different sexual lifestyles.

Among those who experienced a problem in their sexual relationship due to the lack of sexual desire on the part of their sexual partner during the past year, 46% of the men (N = 787) and 31% of the women (N = 363) had masturbated (during the last month; based on combined data from the 1992 and 1999 Finnish surveys). Among those who did not experience a problem with the lack of sexual desire on the part of their sexual partners, 34% of men (N = 580) and 22% of women (N = 987) reported masturbating during the last month.

In 1999 in Finland, 88% of men and 66% of women reported that at least sometimes they experienced orgasm through masturbation. In the younger generations these figures were around 95% for men and 80% for women. In the U.S., about 80% of men and 60% of women reported that they usually or always experienced orgasm when masturbating. The more often people masturbated, the more likely they were to report experiencing orgasm when masturbating (Laumann et al., 1994).

DISCUSSION

This study provided an overview of changes in masturbation habits in different generations born between 1917 and 1980 by using three national sex surveys in Finland and comparable data from Sweden, Estonia, and St. Petersburg (Russia). Our analysis showed how masturbation has varied in different generations in two Western societies (Finland and Sweden) and in two former Soviet societies (Estonia and St. Petersburg), resulting in a social history of masturbation in Northern Europe in the 1900s.

Our findings support the notion that the revolution of sexual knowledge and values that took place in the Western societies in the late 1960s and early 1970s had a major impact on the attitudes and behaviors related to masturbation. Fears about the health hazards of masturbation decreased and masturbation increased considerably from one generation to the next. The observed masturbation trends are consistent with the ideas presented in the public discussion and information on masturbation in the teenage years of each generation.

Some of these trends may be due to increasing social desirability and social acceptability of masturbation during the latest decades (Dubois-Arber et al., 1997). In the later generations it might have been easier to reveal one's own masturbation habits. However, no evidence is currently available that would confirm this assumption. On the other hand, the sex surveys among the general population have provided more valid estimates of life time masturbation prevalence than surveys among adolescents (Halpern et al., 2000). Being honest about one's masturbation habits may be easier for adults than for adolescents.

Some of the increase in masturbation rates could be due to selection bias of the respondents. In order to check the possible impact of such a bias we have taken some measures to assess the validity of the results. One such measure is the comparison of the survey responses to life time abortion rates and national abortion statistics. They matched. In addition, we were able to examine retrospective reports obtained three times from most of the age groups in the Finnish surveys. Adolescent sex education and first sexual experiences of each generation were reported in the same way from one survey to the other. And finally, the responses of men and women to several other questions in the surveys (loving and being loved; the quality of the relationship; the frequency of intercourse, oral sex, anal sex, and erection disorders) were also consistent. These findings indicate that the results presented in this article are at least reasonably valid. (Kontula, 2001; Haavio-Mannila & Kontula, 2001.)

The increasing masturbation rates in Finland are also consistent with some other findings in recent European sex surveys. The age of first intercourse has declined in Western Europe by two years on average since the 1960s (Bozon & Kontula, 1998). At the same time there has been an increase in the frequency of intercourse, the number of sex partners, and the practice of oral and anal sex (Sandfort et al., 1998). The European sexual habits have become more versatile. Masturbation is one indicator of this more general trend.

The 1990s surveys in Finland showed that fears related to masturbation decreased. This was expected on the basis of findings from a national Finnish press study (1961-1991) showing that sexuality and sexual issues have, to a large extent, been brought out from privacy into the open by the media since the beginning of the 1960s (Kontula & Kosonen, 1996). By analyzing the contents of different popular magazines, they observed that sexuality was discussed in greater detail in public through the years 1961-1991. One could argue that the more open and detailed the discussion about sex in public, the easier it is for people to approve of sexuality in its different manifestations.

According to studies of the sexual autobiographies of ordinary people, fears related to masturbation have been common among many generations in Finland, Estonia and St. Petersburg. Several authors of sexual life histories have been afraid of the negative consequences of masturbation after reading warnings in publications or after hearing about them from others. Fears (of becoming insane) and guilt related to masturbation were common especially before the 1970s. Some people explained how they had tried to stop masturbating because of these fears, usually unsuccessfully. Even among women in the youngest generations, feelings of guilt remained common (Kontula & Haavio-Mannila, 1997; Karusoo, 1997; Rotkirch, 2000; Haavio-Mannila et al., 2002).

Due to the restrictive public policy against sexual education and expression in the former Soviet Union, changes in masturbation habits took place in Estonia and especially in St. Petersburg 20 or even 30 years later than in Sweden and Finland. This is consistent with Kon's (1995) estimate that the Russian sexual culture lags about 25 years behind that of the West. The Russian tradition to oppose Western ideas ensures that the border between Finland and Russia is a real cultural border with each side having different views on sexual issues. Another manifestation of this is the double standard in St. Petersburg where people give more sexual freedom in marriage to men than to women (Haavio-Mannila et al., 2001, 104-110; Haavio-Mannila & Kontula, 2002).

Masturbation rates have been much lower in Estonia than in Finland, including teenagers. According to the surveys conducted in schools in Estonia in 1994 and in Finland in 1992, 59% of Finnish boys but only

15% of Estonian boys masturbated at least sometimes. For girls these figures were 40% and 6%, respectively (Papp et al., 1997).

In all areas studied here, men have been more active in masturbation than women. However, gender equality has increased even when it comes to masturbation. In the late 1990s, the masturbation rate of women in Finland was as high as that of men 20 years earlier. Women who had started intercourse at a young age were almost as active in masturbation as their male counterparts (Kontula, 2001b).

Some of the gender differences in masturbation habits can be explained by the fact that boys are socialized more to masturbation by their peers than girls. The sexual autobiographies of Finnish men revealed that older boys showed the younger ones how to masturbate. Women almost completely missed this type of sex education (Kontula & Haavio-Mannila, 1995).

One important finding of the current study is that masturbation does not necessarily decrease during the course of one's life. In fact, the three surveys in Finland show that masturbation remained almost at the same level in every birth cohort from one survey to another. This implies that the masturbation habits, which each generation adopted in its teenage years, tend to remain very similar throughout life, even over a 27 years time span. This tells us how important a generational approach is to understand differences between age groups in sexual attitudes and behaviors. Comprehensive sex education for teenagers would help new generations enjoy their sexuality free from unnecessary fears and anxiety.

Our findings suggest that in the future, more and more elderly people will masturbate as they have grown up in a masturbation-friendly society. Today's results from the elderly population may not be applicable to the older people of the future. Moreover, our findings question the assumption that masturbation markedly decreases with age. Instead, masturbation can be a way of satisfying sexual desire in later life when people have widowed and may experience difficulty finding a new sexual partner.

Some people believe that masturbation represents a compensation for "real" sex that is missing for some reason (Kontula & Haavio-Mannila, 1997). By comparing the masturbation habits of people in different relationships of various durations, it was found that masturbation for most of the respondents was an independent part of their sexual activity. It did not simply compensate for not having enough intercourse. Masturbation increased with time in long-lasting unions. Self-pleasuring seems to have become more and more a means of enhancing sexual satisfaction unrelated to one's relationship status. The same phenomenon was found in the Finnish sexual autobiographies (Kontula & Haavio-Mannila, 1997).

Looking at changes in sexual techniques over time, one can assume that fears about masturbation have had a strong impact on inhibitions with manual sex. As manual sex was considered improper with one's own genitals, manual sex with a partner was likely also affected. This is supported by the fact that at the same time that masturbation has increased, there has been a growth of manual sex with a partner (Haavio-Mannila et al., 2001, 271-273).

Sex surveys, such as the ones presented here, have indirectly promoted active masturbation by revealing that masturbation is a common practice that is not harmful. It has become common practice to encourage men and women with sexual problems to masturbate in order to overcome their inhibitions (Kay, 1992). In addition, people with a high interest in masturbation have been found to be less afraid of intimacy than those with no interest in masturbation (Rinehart & McCabe, 1998).

In conclusion, our findings clearly show that masturbation is linked to the perceptions in a given culture of its nature and consequences during people's teenage years. Masturbation is a safe sexual technique without any risks. Thus, promotion of masturbation is a way to promote sexual health.

REFERENCES

Bozon, M. & Kontula, O. (1998). Sexual initiation and gender: A cross-cultural analysis of trends in the 20th century. In Sexual Behaviour and HIV/AIDS in Europe: Comparisons of National Surveys (Eds. Michel Hubert, Nathalie Bajos & Theo Sandfort). UCL Press, London. pp. 37-67.

Bullough, V. (1987). Technology for the prevention of "les maladies produites par la masturbation." Technology and Culture 28, 4, 828-832.

Dubois-Arber, F., Spencer, B. & Jeannin, A. (1997). Methodological problems in trend analysis of sexual behavior. In Researching Sexual Behavior: Methodological Issues (Ed. John Bancroft). Indiana University Press, Bloomington. pp. 196-212.

Ellis, H. (1910). Auto-Eroticism, Vol. 1 of Studies in the Psychology of Sex. Philadelphia.

Gronow, J., Haavio-Mannila, E., Kivinen, M., Lonkila, M. & Rotkirch, A. (1997). Cultural Inertia and Social Change in Russia. University of Helsinki, Department of Sociology (stencil).

Haavio-Mannila, E., Kontula, O. & Kuusi E. (2001). Trends in Sexual Life Measured by National Sex Surveys in Finland in 1971, 1992 and 1999 and a Comparison to a Sex Survey in St. Petersburg in 1996. Working Papers E 10. The Family Federation of Finland, The Population Research Institute, Helsinki.

Haavio-Mannila, E. & Kontula, O. (2001). Seksin trendit meillä ja naapureissa (Trends in Sexual Life at Home and in the Neighboring Countries). WSOY, Helsinki.

Haavio-Mannila, E. & Kontula, O. (2002). Transition to feminine sexual culture in Northern Europe. *The Journal of Sex Research* (submitted).

Haavio-Mannila, E., Kontula, O. & Rotkirch, A. (2002). Sexual Lifestyles in the Twentieth Century: A Research Study. Palgrave, Hampshire & New York.

Haavio-Mannila, E. & Rotkirch, A. (1998). Generational and gender differences in sexual life in St. Petersburg and urban Finland. Yearbook of Population Research in Finland XXXIV 1997. The Population Research Institute, The Family Federation of Finland, Helsinki, pp. 133-160.

Hall, L. A. (1992). Forbidden by God, despised by men: Masturbation, medical warnings, moral panic, and manhood in Great Britain. *Journal of the History of Sexuality* 2, 3, 365-387.

Halpern, C. J. T., Udry, J. R. & Suchindran, C. (2000). Adolescent male's willingness to report masturbation. *The Journal of Sex Research* 37, 4, 327-332.

Hunt, A. (1998). The great masturbation panic and the discourses of moral regulation in nineteenth–and early twentieth-century Britain. *Journal of History of Sexuality* 8, 4, 575-615.

Kaplan, H. S. (1975). The Illustrated Manual of Sex Therapy. Brunnel/Mazel, New York.

Karusoo, M. (1997). Eesti elulood–Kured läinud, kurjad ilmad (Estonian Biographies–When Cranes Leave, The Weather Turns Bad). Eesti Kirjandusmuseum, Tartu.

Kay, D. S. G. (1992). Masturbation and mental health–Uses and abuses. Sexual and Marital Therapy 7, 1, 97-107.

Kellogg, J. H. (1974). Plain Facts for Old and Young, Plain facts about sexual life. Heritage Press. Buffalo.

Kon, I. S. (1995). The Sexual Revolution in Russia. From the Age of the Czars to Today. The Free Press, New York.

Kontula, O. (2001). Response rate and selection bias in a sex survey: An empirical test. Paper presented in the IUSSP XXIV General Population Conference held in Salvador, Brazil, August 18-24, 2001.

Kontula, O. (2001b). Masturbation in generational perspective. Paper presented in the 44th Annual Meeting of The Society for the Scientific Study of Sexuality (SSSS) held in San Diego, October 25-28, 2001.

Kontula, O. & Haavio-Mannila, E. (1995). Sexual Pleasures–Enhancement of Sex Life in Finland, 1971-1992. Dartmouth, Aldershot, Hampshire, U. K.

Kontula, O. & Haavio-Mannila, E. (1995). Matkalla intohimoon: Nuoruuden hurma ja kärsimys seksuaalielämäkertojen kuvaamana (Along the Way to Passion: The Joy and Suffering of Youth Revealed in Sexual Autobiographies). WSOY, Helsinki.

Kontula, O. & Haavio-Mannila, E. (1997). Intohimon hetkiä: Seksuaalisen läheisyyden kaipuu ja täyttymys omaelämäkertojen kuvaamana (Moments of Passion: The Longing for Sexual Intimacy and Its Fulfillment Described in Autobiographies). WSOY, Helsinki.

Kontula, O. & Kosonen, K. (1996). Sexuality changing from privacy to the open–A study of the Finnish press over the years from 1961 to 1991. Nordisk Sexologi 14, 1, 34-47.

Laumann E. O., Gagnon, J. H., Michael, R. T. & Michaels, S. (1994). The Social Organization of Sexuality. Sexual Practices in the United States. The University of Chicago Press, Chicago and London.

Lewin, B., Fugl-Meyer K., Helmius G., Lalos, A. & Månsson, S-A. (1998). Sex i Sverige: Om sexuallivet i Sverige 1996. (Sex in Sweden: About Sexual Life in Sweden). Folkhälsoinstitutet 11, Stockholm.

Liljeström, M. (1995). Emanciperade till underordning: Det sovjetska könssystemets uppkomst och diskursiva reproduktion (Emancipated Into Resignation: The Birth of the Soviet Gender System and Discursive Reproduction). Åbo Akademis förlag, Åbo.

Michaels, S. & Giami, A. (1999). Sexual acts and sexual relationships: Asking about sex in surveys. Public Opinion Quarterly 63, 401-420.

Money, J. (1999): The sex police in history. *Journal of Gender, Culture, and Health* 4, 4, 269-279.

Money, J. (1985). The Destroying Angel: Sex, Fitness & Food in the Legacy of Degeneracy Theory, Graham Crackers, Kellogg's Corn Flakes & American Health History. Prometheus Books, New York.

Papp, K., Kontula, O. & Kosunen, E. (1998). Teenage sexuality in Estonia and in Finland in the 1990s. Yearbook of Population Research in Finland XXXIV 1997. The Family Federation of Finland, Population Research Institute, Helsinki, pp. 161-172.

Parrinder, G. (1980). Sex in the World's Religions. Sheldon Press, London.

Patton, M. S. (1985). Masturbation from Judaism to Victorianism. *J. Rel. Health* 24, 133-146.

Poolamets, O. (2001). Personal information.

Rinehart N. J. & McCabe, M. P. (1998). An empirical investigation of hypersexuality. Sexual and Marital Therapy 13, 4, 369-384.

Rotkirch, A. (2000). The Man Question–Loves and Lives in Late 20th Century Russia. Research Reports 1/2000. Department of Social Policy, University of Helsinki, Helsinki.

Sandfort, T., Bos, H., Haavio-Mannila, E. & Sundet, J. M. (1998). Sexual practices and their social profiles. In Sexual Behaviour and HIV/AIDS in Europe: Comparisons of National Surveys (Eds Michel Hubert, Nathalie Bajos, Theo Sandfort). UCL Press, London, pp. 106-164.

Sharma, V. & Sharma, A. (1998). The guilt and pleasure of masturbation: A study of college girls in Gujarat, India. Sexual and Marital Therapy 13, 1, 63-70.

Spira, A., Bajos, N. & The ACSF Group (1994). Sexual Behaviour and AIDS. Avebury, Aldershot, Hampshire.

Stolberg, M. (2000). An unmanly vice: Self-pollution, anxiety, and the body in the eighteenth century. Social History of Medicine 13, 1, 1-21.

Tiefer, L. (1998). Masturbation: Beyond caution, complacency and contradiction. Sexual and Marital Therapy 13, 1, 9-14.

Tissot, S. A. (1974). A treatise on the diseases produced by onanism. In The Secret Vice Exposed! Some Arguments Against Masturbation (Eds. C. Rosenberg and C. Smith-Rosenberg). Arno Press, New York.

Unal, F. (2000). Predisposing factors in childhood masturbation in Turkey. European *Journal of Pediatrics* 159, 5, 338-342.

Whorton, J. (2001). The solitary vice: The superstition that masturbation could cause mental illness. *Western Journal of Medicine* 175: 66-68.

Masturbation and Sexual Health: An Exploratory Study of Low Income African American Women

Beatrice "Bean" E. Robinson, PhD
Walter O. Bockting, PhD
Teresa Harrell, PhD

ABSTRACT. In this study we applied research examining the hypothesized benefits of masturbation in dealing with sexual problems to the urgent health crisis posed by the HIV/AIDS pandemic. This is the first study to test the hypothesized relationship between masturbation and HIV risk as predicted by the Sexual Health Model, a sex-positive approach to sexual health developed in response to the need for a more explicit focus on sexuality and relationships in HIV prevention. This is also

Beatrice "Bean" E. Robinson is Associate Professor and Associate Director, Program in Human Sexuality, University of Minnesota Medical School, Department of Family Practice and Community Health, Minneapolis, MN.

Walter O. Bockting is Assistant Professor, Program in Human Sexuality, University of Minnesota Medical School, Department of Family Practice and Community Health, Minneapolis, MN.

Teresa Harrell is Associate Director, International Student and Scholar Services, Adjunct Faculty, Department of Family Practice & Community Health, University of Minnesota, Minneapolis, MN.

Address correspondence to Beatrice "Bean" E. Robinson, PhD, University of Minnesota Medical School, Department of Family Practice and Community Health, 1300 S. 2nd Street, Suite 180, Minneapolis, MN 55454 (E-mail: brobinsn@famprac.umn.edu).

[Haworth co-indexing entry note]: "Masturbation and Sexual Health: An Exploratory Study of Low Income African American Women." Robinson, Beatrice E., Walter O. Bockting, and Teresa Harrell. Co-published simultaneously in *Journal of Psychology & Human Sexuality* (The Haworth Press, Inc.) Vol. 14, No. 2/3, 2002, pp. 85-101; and: *Masturbation as a Means of Achieving Sexual Health* (ed: Walter O. Bockting and Eli Coleman) The Haworth Press, Inc., 2002, pp. 85-101. Single or multiple copies of this article are available for a fee from The Haworth Document Delivery Service [1-800-HAWORTH 9:00 a.m. - 5:00 p.m. (EST). E-mail address: getinfo@haworthpressinc.com].

85

the first study to examine the relationship between several masturbation variables (i.e., masturbation guilt, lifetime masturbation, and current masturbation) and HIV-related sexual behaviors and attitudes in a sample of African American women (N = 239). Data was collected using face-to-face structured interviews as part of the Women's Initiative for Sexual Health (WISH), a randomized, controlled trial of an HIV prevention intervention based on the Sexual Health Model, targeting low income, adult African American women. Contrary to expectations, results showed that participants who reported masturbating were more likely to report having multiple partners, being in a nonmonogamous relationship and engaging in high-risk sexual behaviors. There was no significant relationship between level of masturbation guilt and HIV risk nor between masturbation and consistent condom use or attitudes toward condoms. This study adds to the growing empirical support for associations between sexual health variables and safer sex and argues for a more explicit focus on sexuality in HIV prevention. *[Article copies available for a fee from The Haworth Document Delivery Service: 1-800-HAWORTH. E-mail address: <getinfo@haworthpressinc.com> Website: <http://www.HaworthPress.com> © 2002 by The Haworth Press, Inc. All rights reserved.]*

KEYWORDS. Sexual health, unsafe sex, HIV/AIDS/STD prevention, masturbation, African American women

INTRODUCTION

Women between the ages of 18 and 44 years constitute the fastest growing group of people in the U.S. with HIV/AIDS (O'Leary & Wingood, 2000). Notably, the proportion of AIDS cases among women attributed to heterosexual contact has increased dramatically, rising from 11% in 1984 (Centers for Disease Control & Prevention, 1984), to 34% in 1990 (Centers for Disease Control & Prevention, 1990) and to 41% in 2001 (Centers for Disease Control & Prevention, 2001). Moreover, there is a growing body of evidence documenting associations between safer sex behaviors and sexual factors such as comfort with sexuality and sexual self-esteem (Abraham & Sheeran, 1994; Boldero, Moore, & Rosenthal, 1992). Findings such as these have led many HIV prevention researchers and theorists to acknowledge the need to address the sexual and relationship context of HIV risk in prevention efforts (Ehrhardt, Yingling, Zawadzki, & Martinez-Ramirez,

1992; Kalichman, 1998; Robinson, Bockting, Rosser, Miner, & Coleman, 2002; Robinson et al., in press).

The sexual variable of primary interest in this study is masturbation–both as a behavior, and with regard to the guilt which might accompany it. Throughout history, masturbation has not been recognized as healthy or beneficial by society, religion, or even medicine (Kay, 1992; Patton, 1986). Rather, it has long been considered a "secret" and "unnatural" sin, condemned as a threat to conception in both Judaism and Christianity. In the medical community, masturbation was once considered a cause of mental illness and insanity (18th century), and later a cause of neurosis (late 19th century). Significant social changes in attitudes toward masturbation began with Freud's work on neurosis and his conclusions that masturbation *per se* could no longer be considered pathological but had to be evaluated *vis-à-vis* stages of psychosexual development. Kinsey's statistics revealing that 62% of females and 92% of males had masturbated to orgasm, suggested that masturbation was an important source of sexuality in the life of the average person. Most recently, among psychologists and sexologists masturbation is increasingly recognized as "an essential phase in the normal healthy blossoming of mature sexual responses" (Brecher, cited in Kay, 1993). In addition, it has become one of the most common methods used in the treatment of sexual dysfunction and arousal disorders in both men and women (Kay, 1992).

This relatively new interest in the beneficial effects of masturbation has led researchers to study the relationship between masturbation and other sexuality variables. In samples of female and male college students, frequency of masturbation was positively related to high sex drive and interest but not related to their total number of different sexual experiences (Abramson, 1973; Abramson & Mosher, 1975). In a small elderly sample, frequency of masturbation was positively related to internal locus of control, not having a current sexual partner, and, to a lesser degree, higher sexual knowledge (Catania & White, 1982). Ever having masturbated was associated with being older and having experienced sexual intercourse in a mixed gender college sample (Abramson, 1973). It was also associated with higher self-esteem, marital and sexual satisfaction, more orgasms, greater sexual desire and arousal but not with more frequent sexual activity in a sample of orgasmic military wives (Hurlbert & Whittaker, 1991).

Researchers also began to study the relationship between masturbation behaviors or guilt and sexuality variables with a potential bearing on one's risk of HIV infection. Results from these studies are mixed. On the one hand, in their sample of female and male college students, Leitenberg and colleagues (1993) found no relationship between early masturbation experience and measures of sexual behavior (i.e., whether one had experienced sexual intercourse, the frequency of sexual intercourse, the number of different intercourse partners, the age at which one first experienced intercourse, or the length of one's longest relationship involving intercourse). On the other hand, Choi and colleagues (2000) found that in a sample of young male Korean military personnel, early masturbation was associated with low age at first coitus and a higher incidence of STDs. Davidson and Moore (1994) report that among a sample of women who had experienced sexual intercourse, those who had masturbated differed from those who never had on a number of variables: the former group of women had a higher number of lifetime sexual partners, were less likely to use contraceptives, were more likely to have been diagnosed with an STD, and were more likely to believe they would contract an STD in the future (Davidson & Moore, 1994). Davidson (1984) reported that practicing masturbation was associated with having a higher number of sexual partners and being involved in a serious dating relationship, but also with being less likely to have experienced sexual intercourse.

A few studies have examined the relationship between masturbation guilt and variables related to contraception use and safer sex. Guilt about masturbation has been found to inhibit diaphragm insertion (Gerrard, 1987) and to be more prevalent in women who used no contraception or were abstinent (Mosher & Vonderheide, 1985). In addition, women with high levels of guilt about masturbation experienced more emotional trauma if they contracted a sexually transmitted disease and had greater fear about telling their sex partner than did women with low masturbatory guilt (Houck & Abramson, 1986). In a sample of nurses, masturbation guilt was positively associated with religiosity, and negatively associated with education, overall sexual satisfaction and adjustment, and number of lifetime sexual partners (Davidson & Darling, 1993). In an early report of college women, masturbation guilt was negatively associated with sex experience and masturbation frequency (Abramson & Mosher, 1975).

Research in this area is clearly still developing. Of particular note is that little is known about the masturbatory attitudes and practices of African Americans or other ethnic groups currently demonstrating high rates of HIV and other STDs (e.g., although only 13% of the U.S. female population, African Americans account for 63% of AIDS cases and 67% of HIV infections among women (Centers for Disease Control & Prevention, 2000). Nor is there knowledge about the relationship between masturbation and safer sex variables in these vulnerable populations although other studies have found ethnic differences in sexuality (Laumann, Gagnon, Michael, & Michaels, 1994).

This exploratory study attempts to fill this gap in knowledge by investigating the relationship between several masturbation variables (i.e., ever masturbated, current masturbation and masturbation guilt) and safer sex attitudes and behaviors in a sample of 239 low income, at-risk African American women. We based our hypotheses on the Sexual Health Model which lists masturbation as one of the ten essential components of healthy human sexuality and posits that such sexuality variables are important in determining HIV risk (Robinson, Bockting, Rosser, Miner, & Coleman, 2002). According to the model, if one is more sexually literate, comfortable, and competent, one is also more likely to develop successful, long-term strategies for reducing risk in the context of one's sexual behavior and relationships. Thus, we postulated two hypotheses: (1) women with lower levels of masturbation guilt will be more likely to report behaviors and attitudes consistent with low HIV risk (i.e., consistent condom use, having only one partner, relationship monogamy, low overall risk, and positive attitudes toward condoms); (2) women who report masturbating (during their lifetime or currently) will be more likely to report practicing behaviors and attitudes consistent with low HIV risk.

METHODS

The University of Minnesota (# 9608S11642) and the Centers for Disease Control and Prevention (# 1742) human subjects committees approved this study.

Study Sample

Our sample was comprised of 239 African-American women enrolled in the Women's Initiative for Sexual Health (WISH) study–a randomized controlled trial of a sexual health HIV prevention intervention targeting adult at-risk African American women from the metropolitan area of Minneapolis-St. Paul, Minnesota. (Robinson et al., 2002). The mean age of participants was 34.3 years (SD = 9.6, range = 15-64). Thirty-three percent of the sample was employed full-time, with 49% unemployed and not actively looking for work. Twenty-five percent had less than a high-school education. Forty-one percent of the sample had total household incomes at or below the poverty level, 43% lived in rental properties, and 35% resided in a halfway house, group home or treatment center at the time of pre-testing. Two of the three collaborating agencies through which we recruited for the WISH trial dealt with a chemically dependent clientele, and our sample demographics reflect this: 33% were currently in chemical dependency treatment, and 62% had an alcohol or drug problem currently or in the past. Fifty-one percent of the sample had at least one arrest and, of those, 78% had spent some time in jail or prison.

Procedures

Data for this study were taken from a pre-test measure used in the evaluation of the WISH intervention. Data were collected using face-to-face structured interviews conducted by trained peers and agency staff between July 1997 and August 1998. Participants received a stipend of up to $75 for their participation. Interviews were conducted at places mutually agreed upon between subject and interviewer, usually the participant's home or the offices of one of our collaborating agencies.

Instruments

The two-hour structured interview consisted of 409 questions using mostly fixed choice and/or 5-point Likert-type scales, with a limited number of open-ended questions. For this study, eight variables from the interview schedule were selected for analysis.

Independent Variables–Masturbation

The three masturbation variables were adapted from the work of Exner et al. (1995). Two of these items were dichotomous: "Do you *ever* masturbate?" and "Have you masturbated *in the last 3 months*" (both coded "yes" or "no"). The third item was rated on a 5-point scale and asked how often respondents felt guilty after masturbating (1 = almost never, 2 = occasionally, 3 = about half the time, 4 = often, and 5 = almost all the time).

Dependent Variables–Safer Sex Variables

Attitudes Toward Condoms. This 13 item scale was adapted from Jemmott, Jemmott, Spears, Hewitt, and Cruz-Collins, (1992) and Wingood (1997). Each item was scored 1-5, where 1 = strongly disagree, 3 = neither/not sure, and 5 = strongly agree; higher scores indicate more generally positive attitudes toward condoms. Factor analysis and Cronbach's alpha demonstrated adequate internal consistency (alpha = .75; Robinson et al., 2002).

HIV Risk Behavior Variables. The HIV risk behavior variables were based on the work of Hines, Snowden, and Graves (1998) measuring various aspects of sexual behavior as follows:

1. *Condom Use.* This measure was based on several questions that asked how often the respondent had engaged in vaginal and/or anal sex without a condom during the past 3 months. Items were presented first with reference to a "main" sexual partner and again with reference to "other" sexual partners. Similar to Hines, Snowden and Graves (1998), this variable was dichotomized to represent inconsistent condom use (condom not used every time, coded "1") vs. consistent condom use (condom used every time, coded "2").

2. *Number of Sexual Partners.* This measure was based on questions regarding whether the respondent had additional partners (other than her main partner) over the past 3 months. Those who only reported having a main partner were categorized as not having multiple partners (coded "2") and those who reported having other current sexual partners were categorized as having multiple partners (coded "1").

3. *Monogamy.* This measure was based on items which assessed whether respondents had additional sexual partners besides their main partner in the past 3 months and whether they thought their main partner had sex with someone else other than the respondent in the last 3 months (had no other partners, I suspect s/he had other partners, I know s/he had other partners, don't know). In categorizing the relationship as monogamous or not, all ambiguous responses (e.g., suspecting that he had other partners, indicating "don't know" or "other") were resolved by assigning the variable to its riskiest value: non-monogamous. The variable was constructed using two categories: either one or both has other partners (nonmonogamous sexual behavior, coded "0") or both partners were monogamous (monogamous sexual behavior, coded "1").

4. *Low/High Risk Sexual Behavior.* This variable was created by combining the variables for condom use and monogamy. It was comprised of two categories: high risk sexual behavior (i.e., nonmonogamous, incon-

sistent condom use, coded "1") and low-risk sexual behavior (i.e., celibate; monogamous and used a condom; monogamous and inconsistent condom use; nonmonogamous and used a condom; coded "0").

Statistical Analyses

Due to multicollinearity among the independent variables, multivariate statistical techniques were not appropriate. Thus, independent t-tests were used to examine the relationship between masturbation guilt and the safer sex variables. Chi-square analyses were used to examine the relationship between the categorical masturbation variables and safer sexual behaviors. All analyses were conducted using SPSS 10.1.

RESULTS

The data reported here were collected prior to the administration of the intervention and include the responses of all African American women ($N = 239$) who completed the baseline interview.

Descriptive Statistics For Masturbation and Safer Sex Variables

Sixty-two percent of participants (144/234) indicated they had masturbated sometime during their lives, and 36% (74/208) reported having masturbated in the last three months. Of those who were sexually active, only 14% (23/160) reported consistently using a condom in the last three months. Of those with a sexual partner, 25% (40/162) reported having additional partners, and 37% (62/169) reported being in a monogamous relationship. Sixty-five percent of all participants (153/235) were classified as being in a low-risk relationship (as defined above).

Masturbation Guilt and Safer Sex Behaviors

Table 1 presents the results of t-test analyses comparing the masturbation guilt scores of women with different safer sex behaviors (i.e., with respect to condom use, number of sexual partners, monogamy, and overall risk). Mean guilt scores ranged from 1.4 to 1.8 on a 1 to 5 scale, where higher scores indicate greater levels of guilt about masturbating. No significant group differences in the mean scores for masturbation guilt were observed for any of the four HIV risk behavior measures. Thus, participant's self-reported level of guilt after masturbating was

TABLE 1. T-Test Analyses of the Relationship Between Masturbation Guilt and Four HIV Risk Variables

Sexual Behaviors	N	%	Mean (SD) Masturbation Guilt Score[a]	t (df)	p value	
Condom Use						
Consistent condom use	13	14%	1.5 (1.13)	.625 (91)	.533	ns
Inconsistent condom use	80	86%	1.7 (1.30)			
Number of Partners						
Has only one partner	62	66%	1.6 (1.32)	.153 (92)	.879	ns
Has multiple partners	32	34%	1.7 (1.18)			
Monogamy						
Both partners are monogamous	24	24%	1.4 (.97)	1.363 (52)	.179	ns
One or both has > 1 partner	74	76%	1.7 (1.32)			
Overall Risk						
Low risk	80	58%	1.6 (1.24)	.793 (137)	.429	ns
High risk	59	42%	1.8 (1.37)			

[a]Item scored on a 1-5 point scale, where higher numbers indicate higher levels of masturbation guilt.

not related to their condom use, the number of sexual partners they reported, whether they were in a monogamous relationship, nor their overall level of HIV/STD risk.

Masturbation Behavior and Safer Sex Behaviors

Table 2 presents the results of chi-square analyses comparing the masturbation behaviors (over the respondent's lifetime and in the past three months) of women with different safer sex behaviors (again, with respect to condom use, number of sexual partners, monogamy, and overall risk). Six of the eight group differences were statistically significant. Women who masturbated (during their lifetime or in the last three months) were more likely to report engaging in three of the four unsafe sexual behaviors examined: having multiple partners, being in a non-monogamous relationship and engaging in high-risk sexual behavior. However, in our sample whether a woman masturbated was not related to whether she used condoms consistently.

TABLE 2. Chi Square Analyses of the Relationship Between Masturbation Behavior and Four HIV Risk Variables

Sexual Behaviors	Masturbation Behavior								
	Masturbated in lifetime					Masturbated in past 3 months			
	Yes %	No %	Pearson $\chi^2(1)$	p value		Yes %	No %	Pearson $\chi^2(1)$	p value
Condom Use									
Consistent condom use	13%	16%	.269	.647	ns	16%	16%	.008	1.00 ns
Inconsistent condom use	87%	84%				84%	84%		
Number of Partners									
Has only one partner	67%	89%	9.402	.002	**	61%	87%	12.097	.001 ***
Has multiple partners	33%	11%				39%	13%		
Monogamy									
Both partners are monogamous	27%	54%	12.746	.001	***	20%	49%	12.086	.001 ***
One or both has > 1 partner	74%	46%				80%	51%		
Overall Risk									
Low risk	58%	77%	8.899	.003	**	55%	74%	7.468	.008 **
High risk	42%	23%				45%	26%		

* $p \le .05$
** $p \le .01$
*** $p \le .001$

Masturbation Behavior, Guilt, and Attitudes Toward Condoms

Table 3 presents the results of the t-test analyses comparing the condom attitudes of women with different levels of masturbation guilt (low/high) and different masturbation behaviors (yes/no over their lifetime, and within last 3 months). No significant group differences were observed. That is, women with "lower" levels of masturbation guilt did not significantly differ in their attitudes toward condoms (mean condom attitude score = 3.9) compared to women with "higher" levels of guilt (mean attitude score = 3.7). In addition, the mean condom attitude scores were the same for all groups, regardless of their masturbation behaviors.

DISCUSSION

This is the first study to examine the relationship between several masturbation variables (i.e., masturbation guilt, lifetime masturbation, and current masturbation) and HIV-related safer sex behaviors and attitudes in a low income, African American female sample. Although our review of the literature revealed several findings suggesting that guilt about masturbation was negatively associated with contraception, we did not demonstrate a similar negative relationship between masturbation guilt and the safer sex attitudes and behaviors examined in this study. Thus, our first hypothesis, that women with lower levels of masturbation guilt will be more likely to report behaviors and attitudes consistent with low HIV risk, was not supported. Consistent condom use, having multiple partners, being in a monogamous relationship, or a contextual measure of overall risk were not significantly related to masturbation guilt.

We can think of two reasons as to why this might be the case. First, the contraception behaviors studied in earlier studies and the HIV-related safer sex behaviors examined in our study do not necessarily require similar skills and behaviors. In the one study where guilt feelings associated with masturbation were related to inhibition in inserting a diaphragm, the author speculated that this might be related to a reluctance to handle the genitals (Gerrard, 1987). Although, this same handling issue is relevant for a woman using the female condom, the skills and behaviors required to convince and help a partner put on a male condom (the more common safer sex activity) are quite different from the activities involved in inserting a diaphragm or in masturbation.

TABLE 3. T-Test Analyses of the Relationship Between Masturbation Guilt, Masturbation Behavior, and Condom Attitudes

Masturbation Variables	N	%	Condom Attitude Means (SD)[a]	t(f)	p value	
Masturbation Guilt[b]						
Low guilt	107	80%	3.9 (.56)	1.841	.068	ns
High guilt	26	20%	3.7 (.57)	(131)		
Masturbated in lifetime						
Yes	137	62%	3.8 (.48)	.646	.519	ns
No	84	38%	3.8 (.57)	(219)		
Masturbated in last 3 months						
Yes	68	35%	3.8 (.56)	.600	.549	ns
No	128	65%	3.8 (.53)	(194)		

[a] 13 items, scored on a 5-point scale where 1 = strongly disagree, 3 = neither/not sure, and 5 = strongly agree; higher scores indicated more generally positive attitudes toward condoms.
[b] Dichotomized so that ratings of 1 or 2 (almost never and occasionally) were coded as "low guilt" and ratings of 3, 4, or 5 (about half the time, often, or almost all the time) were coded as "high guilt."

Second, when compared to the literature (Wyatt, Peters, & Guthrie, 1988), the African American women in this study had generally low levels of guilt about masturbation (X = 1.7; only 13% expressed experiencing more than occasional guilt after masturbating). Thus, restricted variance may have affected our ability to demonstrate any relationship between masturbation guilt and safer sex, even if such a relationship existed.

Although masturbation guilt was not related to safer sex behaviors in this study, we found a negative relationship between two masturbation behaviors, lifetime and current masturbation, and three of the four safer sexual behaviors we examined. Participants who reported masturbating (in their lifetime or currently) were more likely to report having multiple partners, being in a nonmonogamous relationship, and being classified as engaging in an overall measure of high-risk sexual behaviors. On the other hand, participants' masturbation behaviors were not associated with another very important safer sex variable, whether or not they used condoms consistently. The direction of these findings was contrary to what we expected to find based on the Sexual Health model (Robinson, Bockting, Rosser, Miner, & Coleman, 2002) and the notion popular among sex therapists that masturbation is uniformly a sign of sexual health. Thus, our second hypothesis, women who report masturbating (during their lifetime or currently) will be significantly more likely to report practicing behaviors and attitudes consistent with low HIV risk, was not supported.

On the other hand, although the findings of this exploratory study were contrary (in the opposite direction) of what we predicted, the negative relationship we found between the masturbation variables and HIV is important and not entirely unexpected. Several studies have found that various masturbation behaviors (e.g., frequency, ever having masturbated, current masturbation, early masturbation experience) were related to sexual variables indicative of high levels of sexual desire, arousal and interest (i.e., high sex drive and interest, higher sexual knowledge, more orgasms, greater sexual desire and arousal; Abramson, 1973; Abramson & Mosher, 1975; Catania & White, 1982; Hurlbert & Whittaker, 1991). This interest and desire could logically be expected to translate into increased, not necessarily safer, sexual behavior.

Even more relevant, consistent with our findings, several studies found negative relationships between masturbation and sexual variables related to safer sex (i.e., having a higher number of sexual partners and being involved in a serious dating relationship (Davidson, 1984), low age at first coitus and higher incidence of STDs (Choi et al., 2000), higher number of lifetime sexual partners, less likely to use contraceptives, more likely to have been diagnosed with an STD and more likely to believe they would contract an STD in the future (Davidson & Moore, 1994). Even more on point, in this special journal issue on masturbation, Pinkerton, Bogart, Cecil, and Abramson (2002), found associations between HIV risk and two masturbation behaviors in a college sample (i.e., early age of masturbation initiation and frequency of masturbation in the last three months). Thus, masturbation may well be associated with some increased HIV risk, perhaps through the mechanism of increased interest and desire. In any case, these findings argue for the importance of continuing to examine the impact of sexuality variables, such as masturbation, on HIV risk.

This study has several limitations. First, our measure of masturbation guilt consisted of a single item. Future researchers should consider using a scale measuring this construct with demonstrated reliability and validity, such as the "Negative Attitudes Toward Masturbation Inventory" (Abramson & Mosher, 1975; Davis, Yarber, Bauserman, Schreer, & Davis, 1998). In addition, future studies should explore the relationship between the more general concept of sex guilt and HIV-related safer sex behaviors. While the concepts of masturbation guilt and sex guilt are related, they are theoretically different; ". . . masturbation guilt is a more specific and narrowly focused example of an affective-cognitive structure or personality mini-script than the more general structure of sex guilt" (Green & Mosher, 1985, p. 3).

Second, our study relied completely on participant self-reports of behavior to an interviewer. Concerns exist regarding the quality of survey measurements of sexual behavior. We know that adults typically underreport many undesirable sexual activities and overreport desirable sexual behavior and attitudes in interviewer-administered surveys (Turner, Miller, & Rogers, 1997; Wagstaff, Abramson, & Pinkerton, 2000). It is possible that the participants who felt guilty about their masturbatory behavior underreported this activity, thus possibly affecting the relationships found between masturbation and safer sex behaviors. In addition, our data on relationship monogamy may also be affected by the inaccuracy of self-report data on their partners. While we have chosen to define monogamy conservatively, it is possible that a respondent believes that her partner is monogamous, when in fact he is not. Certainly, one would have more confidence in our measure if partner characteristics were also based on confidential information obtained from the women's partners, not only on the knowledge of the women themselves. However, the surprisingly high percentage of women acknowledging that their partner was or could be nonmonogamous (58%) suggests that the women in this sample were being realistic, or at least not naively optimistic, about their partner's risk behavior.

Finally, a caution is in order when applying and generalizing these results. It is possible that relationships between masturbation and safer sex variables found in this study are unique to this population of low income, high-risk African American women, one-third of who were enrolled in chemical dependency treatment at the time of the interview. More heterogeneous samples in terms of income, gender, and ethnicity might reveal different associations. While several well-designed studies have demonstrated differences between women and men on masturbation attitudes and behaviors (Davidson & Darling, 1993; Oliver & Hyde, 1993), little is known about masturbation in different ethnic and income groups.

This sample seems to be rather accepting of masturbation in terms of attitudes and behaviors. In addition to the surprisingly low levels of masturbation guilt discussed earlier, they report high levels of current masturbation activity; 36% reported masturbating in the last three months. Although this figure is only slightly higher than figures reported on the masturbation activity of African American women in the National Health & Social Life Survey (32% reported masturbating in the past year; Laumann, Gagnon, Michael, & Michaels, 1994), our participants reported on their activity for a notably shorter period of time (3 months vs. 12 months) and might be expected to have lower, not higher, frequencies because of this shorter time period.

Future studies should continue the investigation of the complex relationships between masturbation and other sexuality variables to safer sex behaviors in diverse populations. We have argued elsewhere that a more explicit focus on sexuality and relationships in HIV prevention is necessary and have presented one framework, the Sexual Health Model, for doing so (Robinson, Bockting, Rosser, Miner, & Coleman, 2002). There is growing empirical support for associations between sexuality variables and safer sex behaviors and attitudes (Coleman, Ross, Miner, & Rosser, 2000; Kraft, Rosser, Robinson, & Bockting, 2001; Rosser et al., 2000). The findings from this study showing relationships between masturbation activity and several safer sex behaviors in a sample of high-risk, African American women study adds to the growing empirical support for associations between sexuality variables and safer sex behaviors and support an explicit focus on sexuality and relationships in HIV prevention. However, the relationship of masturbation to safer sex behaviors needs to be studied further and replicated in different and more heterogenous populations.

ACKNOWLEDGMENTS

The Women's Initiative for Sexual Health (WISH) was a collaborative effort between faculty and staff at the Program in Human Sexuality, University of Minnesota Medical School, Department of Family Practice & Community Health and three community-based organizations: Turning Point, Inc., African American Family Services, and the Minneapolis Urban League. Two other community-based agencies, Eden Programs and La Casa de Esperanza, contributed to the implementation of the intervention and evaluation. In addition, we particularly thank Karen Scheltema for statistical consultation and Anne Marie Weber-Main for editing the manuscript.

The Minnesota Department of Health, AIDS/STD Prevention Services Section, (#1742-634-9027), funded the WISH intervention. The Centers for Disease Control and Prevention, AIDS/STD Prevention Services Section, Program Evaluation Research Branch, funded the evaluation (#U62/CCU513219).

Finally, we thank others who contributed to this project in a myriad of ways: Carol Albright, Candy Ashbach, Denise Black, Judy Brown-Barber, Catherine Butcher, LuTrenze Butcher, Rosetta Chears, Tonya Cherry-Porter, Eli Coleman, Traci Davis, Deb Finstad, Argery Giavasis, Adriann Hawkins, Peter Hayden, Nick

Higgins, Wilhelmina Holder, Ross Johnson, Shantel King, Heather Livingston, Mary Mabry, Salima Majeed, Jasmine Malcolm, Rose McCullough, David McCaffrey, Michael Miner, Christine Moore, Zsame Morgan, Yako Myers, Patricia Nelson, Annette Nicolai, Priscilla Palm, Dianne Patras, John Pina, Maria Scheideggar, Pamela Smith, Deb Smyre, Ebony Starr, Tara Treglowne, Lori Williams, and Manuel Woods.

REFERENCES

Abraham, C. S., & Sheeran, P. (1994). Modeling and modifying your heterosexuals HIV-preventive behaviour; a review of theories, findings and educational implications. Patient Education and Counseling, 23, 173-186.

Abramson, P. (1973). The relationship of the frequency of masturbation to several aspects of personality and behavior. *The Journal of Sex Research,* 9 (2), 132-142.

Abramson, P. R., & Mosher, D. L. (1975). Development of a measure of negative attitudes toward masturbation. *Journal of Consulting and Clinical Psychology,* 43, 4, 485-490.

Boldero, J., Moore, S., & Rosenthal, D. (1992). Intention, context, and safe sex: Australian adolescent's responses to AIDS. *Journal of Applied Social Psychology,* 22, 17, 1374-1396.

Catania, J. A., & White, C. B. (1982). Sexuality in an aged sample: Cognitive determinants of masturbation. Archives of Sexual Behavior, 11 (3), 237-245.

Centers for Disease Control and Prevention (1984). Acquired Immunodeficiency Syndrome (AIDS) Weekly Surveillance Report–United States. Retrieved February 26, 2002, from (www.cdc.gov/hiv/stats/surveillance84.pdf).

Centers for Disease Control and Prevention (1990). AIDS cases by age group, exposure category, and sex, reported in 1989 and 1990; and cumulative totals, by age group and exposure category, through December 1990, United States. Retrieved February 26, 2002, from (www.cdc.gov/hiv/stats/surveillance90.pdf).

Centers for Disease Control and Prevention (2000). HIV/AIDS among African Americans. Retrieved February 26, 2002, from (www.cdc.gov/hiv/pubs/facts/afam.htm).

Centers for Disease Control and Prevention (2001). AIDS cases by age group, exposure category, and sex, reported through June 2001, United States. 13 (1), Mid-Year Edition. Retrieved February 26, 2002, from (www.cdc.gov/hiv/stats/hasr1301/table5.htm).

Centers for Disease Control & Prevention (2001). HIV infection cases by sex, age at diagnosis, and race/ethnicity, reported through June 2001, from 36 areas with confidential HIV infection reporting. 13 (1), Mid-Year Edition. Retrieved February 26, 2002, from (www.cdc.gov/hiv/stats/hasr1301/table8.htm).

Choi, Y. J., Lee, W. H., Rha, K. H., Xin, Z. C., Choi, Y. D., & Choi, H. K. (2000). Masturbation and its relationship to sexual activities of young males in Korean military service. *Yonsei Medical Journal,* 41 (2), 205-208.

Coleman, E., Ross, M. W., Miner, M., & Rosser, B. R. S. (2000). Structure of the Compulsive Sexual Behavior Inventory in homosexual men and its associations with compulsive and unsafe sexual behavior. Manuscript in preparation.

Davidson, J. K. (1984). Autoeroticism, sexual satisfaction, and sexual adjustment among university females: Past and current patterns. Deviant Behavior, 5, 121-140.

Davidson, J. K., & Darling, C. A. (1993). Masturbatory guilt and sexual responsiveness among post-college-age women: Sexual satisfaction revisited. *Journal of Sex & Marital Therapy*, 19 (4), 289-300.

Davidson, J. K., & Moore, N. B. (1994). Masturbation and premarital sexual intercourse among college women: Making choices for sexual fulfillment. *Journal of Sex & Marital Therapy*, 20 (3), 178-195.

Davis, C. M., Yarber, W. L., Bauserman, R., Schreer, G., Davis, S. L (Eds.) (1998). Handbook of sexuality-related measures. Thousand Oaks, CA: Sage Publications.

Ehrhardt, A. A., Yingling, S., Zawadzki, R., & Martinez-Ramirez, M. (1992). Prevention of heterosexual transmission of HIV: Barriers for women. *Journal of Psychology and Human Sexuality*, 5 (1/2), 37-67.

Exner, T., Meyer-Bahlburg, H., Yingling, S., Hoffman, S., Ortiz-Torres, B., & Ehrhardt, A. A. (1995). Baseline interview for Project FIO (The future is ours). Unpublished, Columbia University, Department of Psychiatry, New York, NY.

Gerrard, M. (1987). Sex, sex guilt and contraceptive use revisited: The 1980's. *Journal of Personality and Social Psychology*, 52, 975-980.

Green, S. E., & Mosher, D. L. (1985). A causal model of sexual arousal to erotic fantasies. *The Journal of Sex Research*, 21 (1), 1-23.

Hines, A. M., Snowden, L. R., and K. L. Graves. (1998). "Acculturation, Alcohol Consumption and AIDS-Related Risky Sexual Behavior Among African American Women." Women & Health, 27 (3) 17-35.

Houck, E. L., & Abramson, P. R. (1986). Masturbatory guilt and the psychological consequences of sexually transmitted diseases among women. *Journal of Research in Personality*, 20, 267-275.

Hurlbert, D. F., & Whittaker, K. E. (1991). The role of masturbation in marital and sexual satisfaction: A comparative study of female masturbators and nonmasturbators. *Journal of Sex Education & Therapy*, 17 (4), 272-282.

Jemmott, J. B., Jemmott, L. S., Spears, H., Hewitt, N., & Cruz-Collins, M. (1992). Self-efficacy, hedonistic expectancies, and condom-use intentions among inner city black adolescent women: A social cognitive approach to AIDS risk behavior. *Journal of Adolescent Health*, 512-519.

Kalichman, S. (1998). Preventing AIDS: A sourcebook for behavioral interventions. Mahwah, NJ. Lawrence Erlbaum Associates, Publishers.

Kay, D. S. G. (1992). Masturbation and mental health–uses and abuses. Sexual and Marital Therapy, 7 (1), 97-107.

Kelley, K. (1985). Sex, sex guilt, and authoritarianism: Differences in responses to explicit heterosexual and masturbatory slides. *Journal of Sex Research*, 21 (1), 68-85.

Kelly, M. P., Strassbert, D. S., & Kircher, J. R. (1990). Attitudinal and experiential correlates of anorgasmia. Archives of Sexual Behavior, 19, 2, 167-177.

Kraft, C., Rosser, B. R. S., Robinson, B. E., & Bockting, W. O. (2001). Body mass index, body image, and unsafe sex in men who have sex with men. Manuscript submitted for publication.

Laumann, E. O., Gagnon, J. H., Michael, R. T., & Michaels, S. (1994). The social organization of sexuality: Sexual practices in the United States. Chicago: University of Chicago Press.

Leitenberg, H., Detzer, M. J., & Srebnik, D. (1993). Gender differences in masturbation and the relation of masturbation experience in preadolescence and/or early adolescence to sexual behavior and sexual adjustment in young adulthood. Archives of Sexual Behavior, 22 (2), 87-98.

Mosher, D. L., & Vonderheide, S. G. (1985). Contributions of sex guilt and masturbation guilt to women's contraceptive attitudes and use. *Journal of Sex Research*, 21 (1), 24-39.

O'Leary, A., & Wingood, M. (2000). Interventions for sexually active heterosexual women. In J. L. Peterson & R. J. DiClemente (Eds.), Handbook of HIV prevention (pp. 179-200). Kluwer Academic/Plenum Publishers: New York.

Oliver, M. B., & Hyde, J. S. (1993). Gender differences in sexuality: A meta-analysis. Psychological Bulletin, 114 (1), 29-51.

Patton, M. S. (1985). Masturbation from Judaism to Victorianism. *Journal of Religion and Health*, 24 (2), 133-146.

Patton, M. S. (1986). Twentieth-century attitudes toward masturbation. *Journal of Religion and Health*, 25 (4), 291-302.

Pinkerton, S. D., Bogart, L. M., Cecil, H., & Abramson, P. R. (2002). Factors associated with masturbation in a collegiate sample. *Journal of Psychology and Human Sexuality*. 14(2/3), 103-121.

Robinson, B. E., Bockting, W. O., Rosser, B. R. S., Miner, M. & Coleman, E. (2002). The Sexual Health Model: Application of a sexological approach to HIV prevention. Health Education Research: Theory & Practice, 17 (1), 43-57.

Robinson, B. E., Uhl, G., Miner, M., Bockting, W. O., Scheltema, K., Rosser, B. R. S. et al. (2002). Evaluation of a sexual health approach to prevent HIV among low income, urban, primarily African-American women: Results of a randomized controlled trial. AIDS: Education & Prevention, 14, Supplement A, 81-96.

Rosser, B. R. S., Bockting, W. O., Rugg, D. L., Robinson, B. E., Ross, M. W., Bauer, G. R., & Coleman, E. (2002). A randomized controlled intervention trial of a sexual health approach to long-term HIV risk reduction: I. Results of the intervention on unsafe sexual behavior among men who have sex with men. AIDS: Education & Prevention, 14, Supplement A, 59-71.

Turner, C. F., Miller, H. G., & Rogers, S. M. (1997). Survey measurement of sexual behavior. In J. Bancroft (Ed.), Researching sexual behavior, pp. 37-60. Indiana University Press: Bloomington.

Wagstaff, D. A., Abramson, P. R., & Pinkerton, S. D. (2000). Research in human sexuality. In L. T. Szuchman and F. Muscarella, Psychological perspectives on human sexuality, pp. 3-59, John Wiley & Sons, Inc.: New York.

Wingood, G. (1997). SISTA (Sisters Informing Sisters About Topics on AIDS) Questionnaire. Unpublished, Center for AIDS Research, University of Alabama, Birmingham, Alabama.

Wyatt, G. E., Peters, S. D., & Guthrie, D. (1988). Kinsey revisited, Part II: Comparisons of the sexual socialization and sexual behavior of black women over 33 years. Archives of Sexual Behavior, 17 (4), 289-332.

Factors Associated with Masturbation in a Collegiate Sample

Steven D. Pinkerton, PhD
Laura M. Bogart, PhD
Heather Cecil, PhD
Paul R. Abramson, PhD

ABSTRACT. This study examined masturbation experience (yes/no), frequency of masturbation in the past three months, and age at initiation of masturbation for 223 undergraduates who completed an anonymous survey. Descriptive, correlational, and regression analyses were con-

Steven D. Pinkerton is affiliated with the Center for AIDS Intervention Research, Department of Psychiatry and Behavioral Medicine, Medical College of Wisconsin, Milwaukee, WI.

Laura M. Bogart is affiliated with the Center for AIDS Intervention Research Department of Psychiatry and Behavioral Medicine Medical College of Wisconsin, Milwaukee, WI, and the Department of Psychology, Kent State University, Kent, OH.

Heather Cecil is affiliated with the Department of Psychology, Pennsylvania State University, Harrisburg, Harrisburg, PA.

Paul R. Abramson is affiliated with the Department of Psychology, University of California, Los Angeles, Los Angeles, CA.

This research was supported, in part, by grant P30-MH52776 from the National Institute of Mental Health (NIMH) and by NRSA postdoctoral training grant T32-MH19985. A preliminary analysis of these data was presented at the Society for the Scientific Study of Sexuality Midcontinent Region Annual Conference, Madison WI, May 20-23, 1999.

Address correspondence to Steven D. Pinkerton, PhD, Center for AIDS Intervention Research, 2071 N. Summit Ave., Milwaukee, WI 53202 (E-mail: pinkrton@ mcw.edu).

[Haworth co-indexing entry note]: "Factors Associated with Masturbation in a Collegiate Sample." Pinkerton, Steven D. et al. Co-published simultaneously in *Journal of Psychology & Human Sexuality* (The Haworth Press, Inc.) Vol. 14, No. 2/3, 2002, pp. 103-121; and: *Masturbation as a Means of Achieving Sexual Health* (ed: Walter O. Bockting and Eli Coleman) The Haworth Press, Inc., 2002, pp.103-121. Single or multiple copies of this article are available for a fee from The Haworth Document Delivery Service [1-800-HAWORTH 9:00 a.m. - 5:00 p.m. (EST). E-mail address: getinfo@haworthpressinc.com].

ducted and HIV risk was estimated using a mathematical model. Men were significantly more likely than women to have masturbated and reported a significantly greater mean masturbation frequency. For men, greater frequency of masturbation was predicted by perceived social norms supporting this behavior. For women, frequency of masturbation was best predicted by social norms and lifetime number of sex partners, whereas masturbation experience was predicted by perceived pleasure and lifetime number of sex partners. Women who first masturbated at a younger age were at higher risk for HIV. In sum, this study suggests that social norms, perceived pleasure, and sexual behavior are important mediators of masturbation experience and frequency. *[Article copies available for a fee from The Haworth Document Delivery Service: 1-800-HAWORTH. E-mail address: <getinfo@haworthpressinc.com> Website: <http://www. HaworthPress.com> © 2002 by The Haworth Press, Inc. All rights reserved.]*

KEYWORDS. Sexual behavior, pleasure, masturbation, HIV risk

If prostitution is the world's oldest profession, then surely masturbation is the world's oldest avocation. Nevertheless, the subject of masturbation has received scant attention by researchers and educators and is seldom mentioned in professional journals (Davidson & Moore, 1994). As a result, relatively little is known about the correlates and determinants of this behavior.

Kinsey and his colleagues were among the first to investigate and report on masturbatory practices. Almost all of the men (> 90%) and more than half of the women (> 60%) they interviewed reported having masturbated in the past (Kinsey, Pomeroy, & Martin, 1948; Kinsey, Pomeroy, Martin, & Gebhard, 1953). Not much has changed since Kinsey's pioneering work, although the incidence of masturbation may have increased somewhat. Reported rates of masturbation experience (i.e., ever having masturbated) vary considerably, but studies consistently find significant gender differences, with more men than women reporting masturbatory experience (Abramson, 1973; Arafat & Cotton, 1974; Greenberg, 1972; Knox & Schacht, 1992; Laumann, Gagnon, Michael, & Michaels, 1994; Leitenberg, Detzer, & Srebnik, 1993; Oliver & Hyde, 1993). Surveys of college age men and women suggest that approximately 80 to nearly 100% of men and 45 to 80% of women have engaged in this behavior (e.g., Davidson & Moore, 1994; Leiblum,

Rosen, Platt, Cross, & Black, 1993; Miller & Lief, 1976; Smith, Rosenthal, & Reichler, 1996).

Most studies find that men masturbate more frequently than women (Greenberg, 1972; Jones & Barlow, 1990; Leiblum et al., 1993; Leitenberg et al., 1993; Smith et al., 1996). Again, there is substantial variation among reported rates, but frequencies of about 2 to 4 times per month for women and 4 to 9 times per month for men are typical (e.g., Atwood & Gagnon, 1987; Clifford, 1978; Davidson & Darling, 1989; Mosher & Abramson, 1977). For both men and women, masturbation is usually initiated during adolescence (Arafat & Cotton, 1974; Atwood & Gagnon, 1987; Clifford, 1978; Green, 1985; Miller & Lief, 1976), although some women report first engaging in masturbation while in their twenties, thirties, or later (Clifford, 1978; Davidson & Darling, 1988; Kinsey, 1953; Laumann et al., 1994).

With regard to the relationship of masturbation to partnered sexual behavior, and vaginal or anal intercourse in particular, the "sex drive" theory (which dates back at least to Kinsey) holds that masturbation is largely a substitute for partnered sex. According to this view, masturbation and intercourse are just two of many potential sexual "outlets" into which the supposedly unitary sex drive can be channeled. Men and women who have active partnered sex lives would, therefore, be expected to masturbate less frequently than persons without partners (Greenberg, 1972). Tests of this theory have produced equivocal results. Clearly, some people do masturbate less when they have regular access to a sex partner. For example, nearly half of the college students studied by Arafat and Cotton (1974) reported that "there is no need for masturbation if they have regular sexual activity with a partner." In contrast, when Clifford (1978) tested the "sex drive" hypothesis, she found no association between women's frequency of masturbation and frequency of vaginal intercourse. Instead, "some women reported that an increase in intercourse stimulated an increase in their general sexual awareness and hence led to increased frequency of masturbation" (Clifford, 1978). Likewise, Greenberg (1972) found no relationship between masturbation and intercourse frequency for his sample of college men and women. However, some studies report a positive association between masturbation and intercourse. For example, although there was no relationship between frequency of masturbation and frequency of intercourse among the young men in Abramson's (1973) study, there was a positive correlation between these activities for women. Similarly, in Davidson's (1984) study, college women who reported more frequent masturbation also reported more frequent intercourse.

More recently, the results of the University of Chicago's *Sex in America* survey suggest that masturbation often occurs within a pattern of active sexuality: "the more sex you have of any kind, the more you may think about sex and the more you may masturbate" (Michaels et al., 1994, p. 165). In this study, married people were more likely to masturbate than people who live alone (Michaels et al., 1994).[1] Moreover, cohabitating individuals reported high rates of both masturbation *and* intercourse, and women with partners were more likely to masturbate than women without partners (Laumann et al., 1994). However, despite evidence that masturbation is part of an active sex life, there was not a clear relationship in this study between frequency of masturbation and frequency of partnered sex.

Sexuality researchers, health educators, and other commentators have suggested that masturbation should be encouraged as a safe alternative to higher-risk sexual practices (Davidson & Moore, 1993; Laumann et al., 1994; Richter & Cimons, 1994; Sparrow, 1994). If, indeed, people have a finite sex drive or "sex budget," then channeling sexual resources into masturbation rather than less safe outlets would help to reduce their risk of becoming infected with human immunodeficiency virus (HIV) or another sexually transmitted pathogen. For example, Davidson and Moore (1993) argue that, "masturbation as a means of sexual self-expression has tremendous potential as an option to provide physiological sexual fulfillment, while avoiding high-risk sexual encounters." This option is not widely utilized, however: only 7% of men and 5% of women who participated in the *Sex in America* study listed fear of HIV/AIDS and other sexually transmitted diseases as a reason for masturbating (Michaels et al., 1994). Still, even if masturbation does not necessarily divert sexual energy away from partnered activities, it might help reduce HIV risk. For example, men who masturbate regularly might feel more comfortable handling their genitals and, therefore, more confident in their ability to use condoms correctly. Masturbation with a partner–which can provide a safe alternative to other higher risk, partnered activities–also might be more common among people who masturbate by themselves. These issues have not previously been explored, to our knowledge.

Social influences on masturbation have received little attention in the research literature. Masturbation is generally a solo activity, hidden in secrecy and shame (Abramson & Mosher, 1975; Davidson & Darling, 1993). Still, masturbation *can* be a social activity, as testified to by adolescent "circle jerks" and the popularity of "jack-off clubs" in certain segments of the gay community (Cornog, 1999). Nevertheless, masturbation remains one of the most stigmatized sexual behaviors, so much so that the extensive *Sex in America* survey used pencil-and-paper questionnaires to collect data on masturbation, rather than the face-to-face interviewing technique that was used for *all* other aspects of the sexuality survey (Laumann et al., 1994; Michael, Gagnon, Laumann, & Kolata, 1994).

Although masturbation is usually a private activity, it nevertheless is strongly influenced by social forces (Laumann et al., 1994). One would expect, for example, that individuals who believe that masturbation is an accepted, normative practice in their social group would be more likely to engage in this behavior themselves, or to do so more frequently. We were able to locate only two studies that examined the influence of peer norms on masturbation. The first found no difference in masturbatory frequency between college women who believed they masturbated about as often as their peers and those who believed they masturbated either more or less often (Clifford, 1978). In contrast, the second study found a significant positive relationship between college student's frequency of masturbation and their perceptions of the frequency with which others masturbated (Greenberg, 1972).

Pleasure is another area that often is overlooked in the literature on masturbation. Masturbation can be a source of both physical and psychological pleasure. Conversely, the desire for pleasure can be a motivating force for engaging in masturbation. Yet, the role of pleasure in masturbation is often overlooked in research studies. When Clifford (1978) interviewed 100 college women about their masturbation experience, the most common reason for engaging in this behavior was pleasure. Similarly, "physical pleasure" was the second most common reason that male and female respondents in the "Sex in America" study gave for masturbating (the most common reason was "to release sexual tension") (Laumann et al., 1994). Also, masturbation was rated as more pleasurable than vaginal intercourse in one study of young married women (Hulbert & Whitaker, 1991; cf., Tavris & Sadd, 1975). Despite the evident importance of pleasure in shaping human sexual behavior (Abramson & Pinkerton, 1995), very few studies have examined its relationship to masturbation.

In sum, substantial gaps remain in our knowledge of factors associated with masturbatory behavior. To better understand the determinants of masturbation and their interrelationships, we surveyed college students about their sexual behavior, their beliefs about the masturbatory practices of other students (i.e., social norms), and their perceptions regarding the pleasurability of masturbation. We then examined the relationships of these variables to several masturbation-related outcome measures: ever having masturbated, frequency of masturbation in the preceding three months, and age at initiation of masturbation.

Based on the literature, we expected to find differences between the masturbation practices of men and women. Specifically, we hypothesized that more men would report ever having masturbated and that men would report a greater frequency of masturbation than women. In addition, we hypothesized that individuals who believe masturbation to be pleasurable and socially normative, and who lead active sex lives, would be more likely to have masturbated in the past and to report masturbating more frequently. Because masturbation can help familiarize a person with his or her body, and may increase comfort levels with genital manipulation (Leff & Israel, 1983), we hypothesized that solo masturbation would be positively related to having been masturbated by a partner, and that men who masturbate frequently would be more likely to use condoms during intercourse. Finally, if frequent masturbation is associated with greater overall levels of sexual activity, then we also would expect frequency of masturbation to be correlated with HIV risk, notwithstanding the possibility of increased condom use. We tested this hypothesis using a model-based estimate of HIV risk.

METHODS

Procedure

As part of a larger study, undergraduate students enrolled in a human sexuality course at a large university in the western U.S. were asked to complete an anonymous questionnaire on various sexuality-related topics. The questionnaire, which was administered by the instructor of the class, consisted of 133 items and took approximately 30 minutes to complete.

Participants

The 223 participants ranged in age from 19 to 40 years ($M = 22.2$, $SD = 2.2$). Sixty-five percent ($n = 145$) were women. Thirty-seven percent self-identified as Asian/Pacific Islander, 34% White, 12% Hispanic, 4% African American, 1% Native American, 6% biracial or multiracial, and 6% "other." English was the first language for 70%. Most of the participants (96%) were college seniors and single (97%). Of the single participants, 51% had a steady partner, 12% had multiple dating partners, and 37% were not presently dating anyone.

Participants were asked to classify their sexual orientation as "heterosexual," "gay/lesbian," "bisexual," or "other," with a "decline to state" option. Twenty-four males and 21 females did not answer the sexual orientation question. Of those that did, 93% of the males self-identified as "heterosexual," 6% as "gay," and 2% as "bisexual," whereas 90% of the females self-identified as "heterosexual," 8% as "bisexual," and 1% as "other."

Measures

Eight demographic items were used to assess participant's age, gender, year in school, marital and dating status, racial/ethnic background, sexual orientation, and whether or not English was their first language.

Sexual behavior was assessed with 14 items. Vaginal and anal intercourse were assessed with four questions each. The items measured whether or not respondents had ever engaged in vaginal (anal) intercourse, how many times they had engaged in vaginal (anal) intercourse during the past three months, and how old they were when they first had vaginal (anal) intercourse, and whether they had used condoms for vaginal (anal) intercourse during the past 3 months. The variables for vaginal and anal intercourse were combined to form four variables that focused on vaginal *or* anal intercourse (e.g., the experience variable assessed whether the respondent had ever engaged in either vaginal or anal intercourse). Similar questions–obtained by substituting "masturbation" for "vaginal (anal) intercourse"–were used to assess solo masturbation experience, frequency, at age at initiation. Participants were also asked to rate how pleasurable they thought masturbation was, on a Likert scale from 1 (not at all pleasurable) to 5 (very pleasurable). Finally, participants were asked to indicate the number of partners with whom they had had sex in the past three months and lifetime.

Gender-specific social norms for female masturbation were measured with the following item: "In your opinion, how often does the average female sexually active [college] student masturbate (by herself)?" Response choices ranged from "never" to "more than 7 times per week." A similar question was used to assess gender norms for male masturbation. Both men and women answered both questions, but the main analyses focus on women's perceptions of female masturbation and men's perceptions of male masturbation.

Social desirability was measured with the 10-item version of the Marlowe-Crowne Social Desirability Scale (Fischer & Fick, 1993). A sample true-false item is, "I always try to practice what I preach." The number of socially desirable responses were summed, so that higher scores represent higher levels of socially desirable responding.

A summary HIV risk measure was constructed to estimate the over-all risk level of respondents and to see whether HIV risk is associated with masturbation practices. This risk measure, which is based on a Bernoulli-process model of HIV transmission (Pinkerton & Abramson, 1993, 1998), provides an estimate of the probability that the respondent would become infected with HIV as a result of the sexual behaviors that she or he reported engaging in during the previous three month period. As such, risk estimates range from a minimum of zero to a theoretical maximum of 1.0. Higher risk scores are associated with greater numbers of partners and acts of intercourse, and with less frequent condom use. Because male-to-female transmission is more efficient that female-to-male, women would be expected to be at greater risk than men, given identical sexual behaviors. Students were split into two groups ("low risk" and "high risk") on the basis of this estimate, using the median risk as a cut-off point.

Statistical Analyses

To examine whether students who responded to the masturbation items differed from nonrespondents on any of the participant demographic or background variables (i.e., age, race/ethnicity, gender, year in school, dating status, marital status, and whether the participant was a native speaker of English), we conducted t-test, chi-square, and correlational analyses. Next, we computed descriptive, correlational, and inferential statistics (t-tests, chi-square analyses) for the masturbation variables, explanatory items, and HIV risk estimates to assess whether gender differences existed and to investigate the relationships of the sexual behavior, masturbation norms, perceived pleasure, and HIV risk variables to the three masturbation-related outcome measures: masturbation experience (i.e., "have you ever masturbated?"), frequency of masturbation in the preceding three months, and age at initiation of masturbation. (Respondents who had never masturbated were excluded from the masturbation frequency analyses, rather than being assigned a frequency of zero.)

Logistic regression analyses were conducted to distinguish between participants who had and who had not masturbated, and multiple regression analyses were conducted separately for men and women to identify significant predictors of masturbation frequency in the past three months. Lifetime number of sexual partners, perceived pleasure of masturbation, and perceived social norm for masturbation were used as predictors in both types of regression analyses. These analyses were conducted separately for men and women because the descriptive analyses identified significant gender differences. (Demographic variables were not included in the regressions due to the lack of variability on many of these items, and because of the lack of associations between the demographic variables and the masturbation outcome measures, as summarized in the Results section.)

The masturbation norms of female undergraduates were used in the analyses of the women participant's data, and the masturbation norms of male undergraduates were used in the analyses of the men's data. To further examine potential gender differences in normative beliefs and, in particular, to investigate whether there was a peer-gender by respondent-gender interaction for masturbation norms (e.g., did normative beliefs about male masturbation vary by the gender of the respondent?), we performed a repeated measures ANOVA on the perceived norms variables with peer-gender as the within-subject variable and respondent-gender as the between-subjects variable.

RESULTS

Descriptive statistics for the masturbation variables, explanatory items, and HIV risk estimates are provided in Table 1. Of the 51 men and 110 women who answered the question, "have you ever masturbated?", 2% of the men (n = 1) and 36% of the women (n = 40) reported that they had never masturbated. A chi-square analysis indicated that men and women differed significantly on this variable ($p < .001$).

Because 28% (N = 62) of the 223 main study participants declined to answer the masturbation questions, we conducted additional analyses to determine whether responders and non-responders differed on any of the demographic (age, gender, year in school, marriage status, dating status, race/ethnicity) or non-masturbation-related behavior variables (number of sexual partners, experience and frequency of vaginal/anal intercourse, condom use), or on propensity toward socially desirable responding. Only one statistically significant association was detected: non-respondents were less likely than respondents to speak English as a first language ($\chi^2(1) = 8.72, p < .01$).

TABLE 1. Descriptive Statistics

	Women	Men	
Masturbation experience	64% yes	98% yes	$\chi^2 (1) = 21.73$***
Masturbation frequency	14.2 (20.2)[a]	36.0 (42.2)	$t (60.58) = 3.24$**
Age at masturbation initiation	14.2 (3.3)	13.1 (4.8)	$t (77.40) = 1.18$
Masturbation norms	2.8 (1.0)	3.9 (1.0)	$t (221) = 8.0$***
Pleasurability	3.5 (1.1)	3.6 (1.0)	$t (181) = .64$
Number of sex partners (lifetime)	4.7 (6.3)	6.6 (6.6)	$t (166) = 1.82$†
Number of sex partners (past 3 months)	0.9 (0.8)	1.1 (1.1)	$t (73.54) = .96$
Frequency of intercourse (past 3 months)	19.0 (22.2)	17.4 (22.9)	$t (146) = -.41$
Any condom use (past 3 months)	42% yes	51% yes	$\chi^2 (1) = 2.14$
Any intercourse experience	80% yes	86% yes	$\chi^2 (1) = 1.00$
Age at first intercourse experience	17.5 (2.4)	16.8 (3.1)	$t (147) = -1.54$
Ever been masturbated by partner	81% yes	83% yes	$\chi^2 (1) = .17$
HIV risk estimate (multiplied by 1,000)	.049 (.144)	.001 (.003)	$t (96.13) = -3.26$**

[a] Mean (standard deviation)
† $p < .10$; * $p < .05$; ** $p < .01$; *** $p < .001$

Of the respondents who reported past masturbation, 46 men and 61 women answered the questions, "how many times did you masturbate in the past 3 months?" and "how old were you the first time you masturbated?" As indicated in Table 1, men reported a significantly greater mean frequency of masturbation ($p < .01$). Converting these three-month totals to monthly equivalents, men reported masturbating an average of 12 times per month, whereas women reported masturbating only 4.7 times per month.

Thirty-six participants reported that they could not remember how old they were when they first masturbated. The mean age of initiation for the 36 men and 45 women who provided numerical estimates did not differ significantly by gender. For men, the mean age was 13.1 years, with a range of 7 to 21, whereas for women the mean was 14.2, with a range of 2 to 22. Four women, and no men, reported masturbating prior to the age of 6 (at 2, 3, 4, and 5 years old); when these data were excluded, the mean age of initiation for women increased to 15.2 years, which is significantly older than the mean age at which men first began masturbating (t (75) = -2.68; $p < .01$).

As shown in Table 1, the men's estimates of the frequency of masturbation among other men (perceived norms) were significantly larger than the women's estimates for other women ($p < .001$). There were no other significant gender differences on the explanatory items. As expected, the calculated HIV risk index indicated that men were at significantly greater risk than were the women ($p < .01$).

Additional findings related to the three main outcome variables–masturbation experience, frequency, and age at initiation–are presented separately below. For the overall sample and for women specifically, frequency of masturbation in the past three months was significantly correlated with age at first masturbation ($r = -.31, p < .01$ and $r = -.39$, $p < .05$, respectively) and with ever having masturbated ($r = .39, p < .001$ and $r = .22, p < .05$, respectively). In particular, masturbating at an earlier age was associated with greater masturbatory activities in the past three months. For men, frequency of masturbation was not related to age at first masturbation. As discussed below, nearly all the male respondents reported having masturbated and, therefore, there was insufficient variability to examine the relationship between ever having masturbated and frequency in the past three months.

Chi-square analyses indicated that none of the three masturbation outcomes depended on race/ethnicity (coded as Asian/Pacific Islander, White, Other), or on participant's dating status (dating vs. not dating) or marital status (married vs. not married). Potential differences with regard to sexual orientation were not assessed due to the lack of variability on this item. There were no significant associations between the social desirability measure and any of the masturbation outcomes (see Table 2).

Masturbation Experience

As shown in Table 2, whether or not a woman had masturbated previously was significantly correlated with most of the variables of interest. In particular, women who had masturbated were more likely to: (1) believe that other women masturbate frequently; (2) consider masturbation a pleasurable activity; (3) have greater numbers of sex partners, both in the previous three months and over their lifetimes; and (4) have had intercourse. They were also much more likely to report having been masturbated by a partner.

Logistic regression analyses indicated that, as a set, pleasure, lifetime number of sexual partners, and perceived social norm significantly distinguished between women who had and who had not masturbated

TABLE 2. Correlational Analyses

	Women				Men	
	Experience	Frequency	Initiation		Frequency	Initiation
Masturbation norms	.44***	.62***	−.19		.62***	−.18
Pleasurability	.52***	.26*	−.36*		.27†	0.0
Number of sex partners (lifetime)	.38***	.41**	−.58***		.14	.29†
Number of sex partners (past 3 months)	.35***	.29*			.06	
Frequency of intercourse (past 3 months)	.17	.25†			−.02	
Any condom use (past 3 months)					.30†	
Any intercourse experience	.33***					
Age at first intercourse experience			.05			.12
Ever been masturbated by partner	.38***					
HIV risk estimate	.05	.25†	−.50**		.11	−.30†
Social desirability	.06	−.02	.02		.18	−.08

Notes: (1) Empty cells indicate relationships that were not assessed; (2) Spearman-rho correlations were used to assess the relationships involving masturbation experience, whereas Pearson correlations were used for masturbation frequency and age at initiation; (3) Men's masturbation experience was not analyzed due to homogeneity of responses.
† p < .10; * p < .05; ** p < .01; *** p < .001

(χ^2 (3) = 34.7, $p < .001$). Perceived pleasure and number of partners were significant independent predictors: women who found masturbation more pleasurable and women who had more sexual partners in their lifetime were more likely to report having masturbated. After controlling for other factors in the model, each standard deviation increase in perceived pleasure of masturbation more than tripled the odds of ever masturbating (OR = 3.79, 95% CI = 1.87-11.14), and each unit increment in the number of lifetime sexual partners was associated with a 1.4 greater odds of ever masturbating (OR = 1.55, 95% CI = 1.13-2.14).

Because only one man reported no previous masturbatory experience, there was too little variability to assess the relationship of the experience variable to the other variables of interest.

Frequency of Masturbation

For women, frequency of masturbation was significantly correlated with masturbation norms, number of sex partners (both lifetime and in the past three months), and perceived pleasurability (Table 2). As with the experience variable, there was a trend associating greater intercourse frequency with greater frequency of masturbation. For men, there was a significant correlation between masturbation frequency and normative perceptions of masturbation among other men and positive trends associating masturbation frequency with pleasurability and condom use.

Multiple regression analyses were performed separately for women and men to identify predictors of frequency of masturbation in the past three months. The following potential predictor variables were entered into the model: number of lifetime sex partners, perceived pleasure of masturbation, and gender-specific masturbation norms. The regression model for women was significant ($F(3,53) = 16.7$, $p < .0001$) and accounted for 49% of the variance in reported frequency of masturbation. Perceived social norm ($\beta = .58$, $t = 5.48$, $p < .05$) and sexual partners ($\beta = .27$, $t = 2.58$, $p < .05$) were significant independent predictors of masturbation frequency ($p < .001$). The model for men also was significant ($F(3,41) = 8.5$, $p < .001$) and captured 38% of the variance. Perceived social norm ($\beta = .61$, $t = 4.49$, $p < .001$) was a significant predictor of masturbation frequency for men ($p < .001$).

Age at Initiation of Masturbation

Women who first masturbated at a younger age were more likely to perceive it as pleasurable ($p < .05$) and to report more lifetime sex partners ($p < .001$), but age at initiation of masturbation was not significantly associated with either masturbation norms or age at first intercourse. For men, age at masturbation initiation was marginally associated with lifetime number of sex partners, such that earlier age of initiation was correlated with smaller numbers of partners.

HIV Risk

HIV risk estimates were calculated for the 49 men and 97 women who provided complete sexual behavior data. The mean HIV risk was significantly greater for women than for men ($p < .01$), as indicated in Table 1. A similar result was obtained when the analysis was restricted to men and women who reported beginning sexual activity in the past three months (men: N = 49, mean risk*1000 = 0.001; women: N = 80, mean risk*1000 = 0.059; $p < .01$).

Results of the correlational analysis are presented in Table 2. For women, greater HIV risk was significantly associated with earlier age of masturbation initiation and marginally associated with frequency of masturbation in the past three months. For men, earlier age of initiation was marginally associated with higher risk, but risk was not significantly associated with masturbation frequency.

Gender Differences in Social Norms

The main effect of the repeated measures ANOVA for perceived norms was significant, indicating that participants believed that male college students masturbated more frequently than female college students ($M = 4.13$ vs. $M = 2.80$, respectively; $F(1,219) = 296.32$, $p < .001$). This main effect was qualified by a norm by gender interaction which indicated that female ($M = 2.76$) and male ($M = 2.85$) participants perceived the female norm similarly, but female participants ($M = 4.38$) thought that male college students masturbated more often than did male participants ($M = 4.38$ vs. $M = 3.87$, respectively; $F(1,219) = 176.95, p < .001$).

DISCUSSION

This study examined factors that influence the masturbation practices of a sample of college students. Almost all the men (98%) and a majority of the women (64%) had masturbated in the past. Both men and women reported frequent masturbation, with men averaging 36 times and women 14.2 times in the past three months. These frequencies are higher than reported in most studies and may reflect greater truthfulness on the part of this sample, which was drawn from a senior-level college sexuality course, or perhaps their relatively young age. Men reported masturbating significantly more often than women, in accordance with prior research (Atwood & Gagnon, 1987; Knox & Schacht, 1992; Laumann et al., 1994; Leiblum et al., 1993; Leitenberg et al., 1993; Smith et al., 1996).

For both men and women, the regression models captured a substantial proportion of the variability in masturbation experience and frequency, although the correlates and predictors of masturbation varied by gender. For men, frequency of masturbation in the past three months was best predicted by the extent to which respondents believed that their male peers masturbated frequently (perceived social norms). There also was a trend toward greater frequency of masturbation among men who believed that masturbation was pleasurable. For women, frequency of masturbation was best predicted by social norms and lifetime number of sex partners. Masturbation frequency among women also was correlated with perceived pleasure and (marginally) with frequency of intercourse. Similarly, women's past masturbation experience was best predicted by a regression model that included perceived pleasure of masturbation and number of sex partners. These results suggest that social norms, perceived pleasure, and sexual behavior items can provide a useful framework in which to examine patterns of masturbation in women and men. They also suggest that the relative importance of these constructs may differ by gender.

Our results do not provide support for the finite "sex drive" hypothesis that frequency of masturbation and intercourse should be inversely related, so that the more masturbation one engages in, the less intercourse he or she should have. Indeed, in this study women who masturbate are more likely to have had intercourse. Moreover, compared to women who masturbate less often, those who masturbate frequently also engage in intercourse more frequently and have more sex partners. Similarly, Robinson, Bockting, and Harrell in this volume of *Journal of Psychology and Human Sexuality* report positive relationships between masturbation and having multiple partners, as well as other sexual activities associated with increased risk for HIV and other sexually transmitted diseases, for a sample of low-income African American women. Frequency of masturbation may be a good indicator of overall sexual interests because it is not partner dependent and because it symbolizes and engages sexual feelings about the self. Therefore, it is not surprising that masturbation is correlated with frequency of intercourse, number of partners, and other measures of sexual activity. Our findings for women are thus consistent with those reported in the *Sex in America* study, which suggested that masturbation often occurs within a pattern of heightened overall sexual activity (Michaels et al., 1994; Laumann et al., 1994). However, we did not observe any evidence of this pattern for men. Whereas for women, incidence and frequency of masturbation may be associated with heightened sexual interest, nearly all the men in our sample reported having masturbated, with a mean frequency that was significantly greater than that reported by the women. Thus, masturbation—even frequent masturbation—does not seem to be a marker for increased sexual interest among men as it is for women.

The HIV risk estimates suggest that women who begin masturbating at a younger age are at greater risk for HIV. This result is not surprising, given that younger age of initiation also was significantly associated with greater numbers of sex partners. In addition, there was a trend toward higher HIV risk for women who report more frequent masturbation. The finding is in direct contrast to theories that propose masturbation as a substitute for higher risk activities (Davidson & Moore, 1993). For women, masturbation is clearly *not* being used as a substitute for intercourse and, therefore, cannot be assumed to decrease HIV risk on that basis. HIV risk was also marginally associated with age of initiation for men. As with the women, it appears that this relationship was mediated by the greater number of partner reported by earlier initiators.

However, we also found that women who had masturbated by themselves were more likely to have also been masturbated by a partner and that men who masturbated frequently were (marginally) more likely to have used condoms in the past three months, as would be predicted if masturbation helped them feel more comfortable with genital manipulation. This suggests that masturbation may be positively associated with behaviors that could help to reduce HIV risk. (For women, HIV risk would be reduced to the extent that masturbation with a partner were in lieu of intercourse or another higher risk activity.) Thus, although men and women who masturbate frequently might be at greater risk for HIV due to greater sex drive, it is possible that the practice of masturbation nevertheless has a positive effect on their risk (that is, they might have been at even higher risk without masturbation).

Masturbation norms were a significant predictor of masturbation frequency for both men and women. Respondents who reported frequent masturbation tended to believe their same sex peers also masturbated frequently. Obviously, the belief that others masturbate normalizes this behavior and thereby makes it more acceptable (Cialdini & Trost, 1998). An interesting gender interaction was noted in participants' perceptions of the frequency with which other men and women masturbate. In particular, although participants believed that men masturbate more frequently than do women, on average, female participants' estimates of the frequency with which male college students masturbate was significantly larger than male participants' estimates. In a related study, Clark (1999) found that men overestimated women's masturbation frequency more than women overestimated men's. It is not clear what influence, if any, cross-gender perceptions might have on respondents' behaviors.

Although this study provides valuable insight into masturbation, several limitations should be noted. First, the results were obtained from a convenience sample of college students and, therefore, care should be exercised when generalizing its conclusions. Moreover, the students were recruited from a human sexuality course and might, therefore, be expected to hold more permissive attitudes toward sex than the average student. Second, as many as 28% of respondents did not answer the masturbation items on the questionnaire, and small sample sizes may have limited the power of this study to detect significant effects. Thus, the obtained results may over- or underestimate the frequency of this activity even within this sample. Third, the student's behavior was assessed via a self-report measure, which may not accurately reflect their actual behavior. Finally, "masturbation" was not explicitly defined in the survey instrument. Presumably, respondents interpreted this term to mean self-stimulation to orgasm. However, the possibility of misinterpretations cannot be completely discounted. A similar concern about terminology applies to the question that asked whether respondents had ever "been masturbated by a partner," which could include stimulation to orgasm or simply foreplay.

In sum, this study suggests that social norms, perceived pleasure, and sexual behavior are important mediators of masturbation experience and frequency. More research is needed to expand these results to other populations, to elucidate how masturbation interacts with these constructs and others that may be relevant to masturbatory practices (such as attitudes, personality traits, and early sexual experiences), and to assess what role, if any, masturbation might play in encouraging safer sexual practices among people at-risk for sexually transmitted infections.

REFERENCES

Abramson, P. R. (1973). The relationship of the frequency of masturbation to several aspects of personality and behavior. *Journal of Sex Research, 9*, 132-142.

Abramson, P. R., & Mosher, D. L. (1975). Development of a measure of negative attitudes toward masturbation. *Journal of Clinical and Consulting Psychology, 43*, 485-490.

Abramson, P. R., & Pinkerton, S. D. (1995). *With pleasure: Thoughts on the nature of human sexuality*. New York: Oxford University Press.

Arafat, I., & Cotton, W. L. (1974). Masturbation practices of males and females. *Journal of Sex Research, 10*, 293-307.

Atwood J. D., & Gagnon, J. H. (1987). Masturbatory behavior in college youth. *Journal of Sex Education and Therapy, 13*, 35-42.

Cialdini, R. B., & Trost, M. R. (1998). Social influence, social norms, conformity, and compliance. In D. G. Gilbert, S. T. Fiske, & G. Linzey (Eds.), *The handbook of social psychology, Vol 2, 4th Ed.* New York: McGraw Hill; pp. 151-192.

Clark, C. (1999). Gender, correlates, and perceptions of masturbation frequency. Presented at the 1999 Society for the Scientific Study of Sexuality Midcontinent Region Annual Conference, Madison WI, May 20-23, 1999.

Clifford, R. (1978). Development of masturbation in college women. *Archives of Sexual Behavior, 7,* 559-573.

Cornog, M. (1999). The circle game: Social masturbation for young and old(er). Presented at the 1999 Society for the Scientific Study of Sexuality Midcontinent Region Annual Conference, Madison WI, May 20-23, 1999.

Davidson, J. K. S., & Darling, C. A. (1988). Changing autoerotic attitudes and practices among college females: A two-year follow-up study. *Adolescence, 23,* 773-792.

Davidson, J. K., & Darling, C. A. (1993). Masturbation guilt and sexual responsiveness among post-college-age women: Sexual satisfaction revisited. *Journal of Sex and Marital Therapy, 19,* 289-300.

Davidson, J. K., Sr., & Moore, N. B. (1994). Masturbation and premarital sexual intercourse among college women: Making choices for sexual fulfillment. *Journal of Sex and Marital Therapy, 20,* 178-199.

Davis, C. M., Blank, J., Lin, H.-Y., & Bonillas, C. (1996). Characteristics of vibrator use among women. *Journal of Sex Research, 33,* 313-320.

Fischer, D. G., & Fick, C. (1993). Measuring social desirability: Short forms of the Marlowe-Crowne social desirability scale. *Educational and Psychological Measurement, 53,* 417-424.

Green, V. (1985). Experiential factors in childhood and adolescent sexual behavior: Family interaction and previous sexual experiences. *Journal of Sex Research, 21,* 157-182.

Greenberg, J. S. (1972). The masturbatory behavior of college students. *Psychology in the Schools, 9,* 427-432.

Houck, E. L., & Abramson, P. R. (1986). Masturbatory guilt and the psychological consequences of sexually transmitted diseases among women. *Journal of Research in Personality, 20,* 267-275.

Hulbert, D. F., & Whitaker, K. E., (1991). The role of masturbation in marital and sexual satisfaction: A comparative study of female masturbators and nonmasturbators. *Journal of Sex Education and Therapy, 17,* 272-282.

Jones, J. C., & Barlow, D. H. (1990). Self-reported frequency of sexual urges, fantasies and masturbatory fantasies in heterosexual males and females. *Archives of Sexual Behavior, 19,* 269-279.

Kinsey, A. C., Pomeroy, W. B., & Martin, C. E. (1948). *Sexual behavior in the human male.* Philadelphia, PA: Saunders.

Kinsey, A. C., Pomeroy, W. B., Martin, C. E., & Gebhard, P. H. (1953). *Sexual behavior in the human female.* Philadelphia, PA: Saunders.

Knox, D., & Schacht, C. (1992). Sexual behaviors of university students enrolled in a human sexuality course. *College Student Journal, 26,* 38-40.

Laumann, E. O., Gagnon, J. H., Michael, R. T., & Michaels, S. (1994). *The social organization of sexuality: Sexual practices in the United States.* Chicago: University of Chicago Press.

Leff, J. J., & Israel, M. (1983). The relationship between mode of female masturbation and achievement of orgasm in coitus. *Archives of Sexual Behavior, 12*, 227-236.

Leiblum, S. R., Rosen, R. C., Platt, M., Cross, R. J., & Black, C. (1993). Sexual attitudes and behavior of a cross-sectional sample of United States medical students: Effects of gender, age, and year of study. *Journal of Sex Education and Therapy, 19*, 235-245.

Leitenberg, H., Detzer, M. J., & Srebnik, D. (1993). Gender differences in masturbation and the relation of masturbation experience in preadolescence and/or early adolescence to sexual behavior and sexual adjustment in young adulthood. *Archives of Sexual Behavior, 22*, 87-98.

Messiah, A., Blin, P., & Fiche, V. (1995). Sexual repertoires of heterosexuals: Implications for HIV/sexually transmitted disease risk and prevention. *AIDS, 9*, 1357-1365.

Michael, R. T., Gagnon, J. H., Laumann, E. O., & Kolata, G. (1994). *Sex in America: A Definitive survey.* Boston: Little Brown.

Miller, W. R., & Lief, H. I. (1976). Masturbatory attitudes, knowledge, and experience: Data from the Sex Knowledge and Attitude Test (SKAT). *Archives of Sexual Behavior, 5*, 447-467.

Mosher, D. L., & Abramson, P. R. (1977). Subjective sexual arousal to films of masturbation. *Journal of Clinical and Consulting Psychology, 45*, 796-807.

Oliver, M. B., & Hyde, J. S. (1993). Gender differences in sexuality: A meta-analysis. *Psychological Bulletin, 114*, 29-51.

Pinkerton, S. D. & Abramson, P. R. (1993). Evaluating the risks: A Bernoulli process model of HIV infection and risk reduction. *Evaluation Review, 17*, 504-528.

Pinkerton, S. D. & Abramson, P. R. (1998). The Bernoulli-process model of HIV transmission: Applications and implications. In D. R. Holtgrave (ed.), *Handbook of economic evaluation of HIV prevention programs.* New York: Plenum Press.

Reading, A. E., & Wiest, W. M. (1984). An analysis of self-reported sexual behavior in a sample of normal males. *Archives of Sexual Behavior, 13*, 69-83.

Reinholtz, R. K., & Muehlenhard, C. L. (1995). Genital perceptions and sexual activity in a college population. *The Journal of Sex Research, 32*, 155-165.

Richter P., & Cimons, M. (1994). Clinton fires surgeon general over new flap. *Los Angeles Times*, December 10, page A1.

Robinson, B. E., Bockting, W., & Harrell, T. (2002). Masturbation and sexual health: An exploratory study of low income African American women. *Journal of Psychology and Human Sexuality.* 14(2/3), 85-102.

Smith, A. M., Rosenthal, D. A., & Reichler, H. (1996). High schooler's masturbatory practices: Their relationship to sexual intercourse and personal characteristics. *Psychological Reports, 79*, 499-509.

Sparrow, M. (1994). Masturbation and safer sex: Clinical, historical and social issues. *Venereology, 7*, 164-169.

Tavris, C. & Sadd, S. (1975). *The* Redbook *report on female sexuality: 100,000 married women disclose the good news about sex.* New York: Delacorte.

Wilson, S. M., & Medora, N. P. (1990). Gender comparisons of college student's attitudes toward sexual behavior. *Adolescence, 25*, 615-627.

Using Masturbation in Sex Therapy: Relationships Between Masturbation, Sexual Desire, and Sexual Fantasy

Brian D. Zamboni, PhD
Isiaah Crawford, PhD

ABSTRACT. Masturbation may be useful in treating hypoactive sexual desire disorder. To examine this possibility, the current study examined the relationships between masturbation, sexual desire, sexual fantasy, and dyadic sexual activity. The relationships between masturbation and other constructs were also examined: overall sexual dysfunction, relationship satisfaction, life stress, and sexual attitudes. Mediational analyses suggest several causal pathways between masturbatory desire, masturbatory frequency, sexual fantasy, sexual desire, and sexual activity. Developing a model of masturbation may help illustrate its role in sexual functioning and highlight its potential role in sex therapy. *[Article copies available for a fee from The Haworth Document Delivery Service: 1-800-HAWORTH. E-mail address: <getinfo@haworthpressinc.com> Website: <http://www.HaworthPress.com> © 2002 by The Haworth Press, Inc. All rights reserved.]*

KEYWORDS. Masturbation, sexual desire, sexual fantasy, sex therapy

---

Brian D. Zamboni is affiliated with the Program in Human Sexuality, University of Minnesota.

Isiaah Crawford is affiliated with Loyola University, Chicago, IL.

[Haworth co-indexing entry note]: "Using Masturbation in Sex Therapy: Relationships Between Masturbation, Sexual Desire, and Sexual Fantasy." Zamboni, Brian D., and Isiaah Crawford. Co-published simultaneously in *Journal of Psychology & Human Sexuality* (The Haworth Press, Inc.) Vol. 14, No. 2/3, 2002, pp. 123-141; and: *Masturbation as a Means of Achieving Sexual Health* (ed: Walter O. Bockting and Eli Coleman) The Haworth Press, Inc., 2002, pp. 123-141. Single or multiple copies of this article are available for a fee from The Haworth Document Delivery Service [1-800-HAWORTH 9:00 a.m. - 5:00 p.m. (EST). E-mail address: getinfo@haworthpressinc.com].

123

Masturbation is an integral part of human sexuality, but few empirical studies have been devoted to this topic. This neglect is probably due to a long history of strong social and religious prohibitions against masturbation (Patton, 1985). Indeed, masturbation has been viewed as an unnatural, sinful act because it does not lead to procreation and because it was presumed to cause a variety of diseases (Patton, 1985). No scientific evidence supports the notion that masturbation is harmful (Renshaw, 1981). Research debunks such myths and shows that masturbation is not harmful (e.g., Kelly, Strassberg, & Kircher, 1990; Leitenberg, Detzer, & Srebnik, 1993).

Although masturbation has not been the central focus of many studies, clinicians often view masturbation as having numerous benefits in the course of normal sexual development and in sex therapy. Masturbation is seen as a way of learning about one's body and sexual responses (Renshaw, 1981). The techniques that can be used to treat premature ejaculation (or simply to postpone a man's ejaculation) are essentially variants of masturbatory activity, and these techniques have high success rates (Kolodny, 1981). Masturbation is also an important aspect of treating female orgasmic disorder (Hurlbert & Apt, 1995; Kelly et al., 1990). Women who have positive attitudes toward masturbation and who masturbate may be more likely to experience satisfactory orgasms than women who do not (Kelly et al., 1990). Most research supports the notion that masturbation may help treat and prevent sexual dysfunctions, but one study has reported that masturbation did not appear to lead to fewer sexual complaints later in life (Leitenberg et al., 1993).

Masturbation appears to be useful in sex therapy for some sexual disorders, but can masturbation be used to treat sexual desire disorders? Recent treatment studies of hypoactive sexual desire disorder have raised this possibility.

MASTURBATION, SEXUAL DESIRE, AND SEXUAL FANTASY

Hypoactive sexual desire disorder (HSDD), a lack of sexual desire, is the most common presenting complaint at sexual dysfunction clinics (Beck, 1995; Donahey & Carroll, 1993). Although masturbation seems to be beneficial in the treatment of premature ejaculation and female orgasm disorder, its relationship to sexual desire has not been studied extensively. Orgasm consistency training, also known as the coital alignment technique, is a therapeutic intervention for couples with HSDD (Hurlbert, 1993). In using this technique, the dyad engages in specific sexual behaviors to produce an orgasm on a regular basis. Thus, the ability to consistently achieve orgasms has been successfully used to treat HSDD (Hurlbert, 1993). If masturbation leads to more orgasms for women (Kelly et al., 1990) and consistent orgasms can be used to treat HSDD (Hurlbert, 1993), then masturbation could play an important role in treating HSDD. Similarly, if individuals know how to masturbate themselves and their partners, they may be less likely to develop HSDD. Of course, the etiology of HSDD appears to be diverse (Beck, 1995; Rosen & Leiblum, 1995) and masturbation may constitute only one part of the treatment plan. Only one known study supports the notion that masturbation could be used to treat sexual desire. A nonclinical sample of married women who have experienced masturbatory orgasm reported more orgasms and higher levels of sexual desire when compared to a demographically matched sample of women who had never experienced masturbatory orgasm (Hurlbert & Whittaker, 1993). Women who had experienced masturbatory orgasm also reported greater levels of self-esteem, sexual satisfaction, and sexual arousability (Hurlbert & Whittaker, 1993). The results suggest that teaching guided masturbation could lead to consistent orgasms, which could increase sexual desire. This is one study, and clearly more research on the relationship between masturbation and dyadic sexual desire is needed. To understand whether or not masturbation can be useful in treating HSDD, the relationship between masturbation and sexual desire in a nonclinical sample must be examined.

The relationship between masturbation and sexual fantasy also needs to be closely examined. A lack of sexual fantasies must be present for the diagnosis of HSDD to be made according to the fourth edition of the Diagnostic Statistical Manual for Mental Disorders (American Psychiatric Association, 1994). Thus, sexual fantasy is believed to precede sexual desire. Pelletier and Herold (1988) have shown that sexual fantasies and masturbation often co-occur and that such fantasies are diverse. Individuals with HSDD have been shown to have fewer sexual fantasies than individuals without HSDD (e.g., Nutter & Condron, 1985). Lower levels of sexual fantasies appear to be associated with lower levels of sexual desire, which should be associated with less masturbation. Unexpectedly, Nutter and Condron (1985) found that men with HSDD masturbated more than a control group. The men with HSDD may have been attempting to increase their sexual desire by masturbating (Nutter & Condron, 1985). Thus, the relationship between masturbation and sexual fantasy also requires clarification. High levels of sexual fantasies should lead to a greater desire to masturbate, which should lead to the act itself.

Jones and Barlow (1990) found that men who had dyadic sex more often also masturbated more and used sexual fantasies more during these activities. By contrast, women currently engaged in dyadic sex appeared to have fewer sexual fantasies; women not engaged in dyadic sex masturbated more (Jones & Barlow, 1990). Other research supports the idea that men who are more sexually active also have more sexual fantasies during masturbation (Campagna, 1985-86). The findings suggest that masturbation has a different function for men and women. For women, masturbation may not complement their sexuality when they are sexually involved with someone. Men may masturbate more because they have higher levels of sexual desire. Unfortunately, sexual desire was not assessed and masturbation was not of central interest (Jones & Barlow, 1990).

Differences in Masturbation by Sex, Ethnicity, and Religion

Due to the limited nature of research on masturbation, relatively few descriptive or inferential facts can be delineated with regard to the topic. Nonetheless, the existing research has described sex differences in masturbation, ethnic/racial differences in masturbatory activity, and religious differences in attitudes toward masturbation. Oliver and Hyde (1993) conducted a meta-analysis on sex differences with respect to sexual behaviors and attitudes. The largest sex difference in terms of sexual behavior concerned masturbation. Men engage in masturbation more frequently than women (Oliver & Hyde, 1993), a finding that also has been reported in subsequent studies (e.g., Laumann, Gagnon, Michael, & Michaels, 1994; Meston, Trapnell, & Gorzalka, 1996). Men may masturbate approximately five times per month, although individual differences can lead to a range of zero to 80 times per month (Leitenberg et al., 1993; Reading & Wiest, 1984). Typical women appear to masturbate about once a month (Leitenberg et al., 1993). Due to socialization forces or anatomical differences, women may not find masturbation as pleasurable or acceptable compared to men (see Leitenberg et al., 1993). Women are not encouraged to explore or learn about their sexuality as much as men. In addition, women's genitals are more covert and less likely to receive easy, direct sexual stimulation.

In terms of the relationship between ethnicity/race and masturbation, one study has indicated that non-Asian Canadian college students masturbated more often than Asian students at the same school (Meston et al., 1996). This difference may reflect differences in cultural norms, although the finding could also reflect under-reporting on the part of Asian participants (Meston et al., 1996). African-Americans also appear to masturbate less often than European-Americans (Laumann et al., 1994). The relationship between religion and masturbation also has been examined. Like the historical religious view of masturbation as sinful (Patton, 1985), more recent research has found that individuals who attend religious services more often are more likely to perceive masturbation as unhealthy or sinful and to feel guilty for masturbating (Davidson, Darling, & Norton, 1995). Overall, these results suggest that religious ethnic minority women may be less likely to respond well to sex therapy techniques that involve masturbation, possibly making it difficult to overcome sexual difficulties (e.g., HSDD, orgasm disorder).

The Current Study

Compared to most of the prior studies on masturbation, this study employed a larger sample size and a wider range of psychometrically sound scales. The current study had two objectives. First, this study sought to examine the relationship between masturbation, sexual fantasy, sexual desire, and dyadic sexual activity. The hypothesized relationships between these variables are conceptually illustrated in Figure 1 and are described below.

Hypothesis I: Masturbatory desire will mediate the relationship between sexual fantasy and masturbatory frequency. Sexual fantasies should lead to the desire to masturbate, which should lead to masturbation.

Hypothesis II: Dyadic sexual desire will mediate a link between sexual fantasy and dyadic sexual activity. Because of the predominantly interpersonal nature of sexual activity, sexual fantasy should lead to dyadic sexual desire and, in turn, dyadic sexual activity.

Hypothesis III: Dyadic sexual desire will mediate the relationship between masturbatory frequency and dyadic sexual activity. If masturbation is employed in sex therapy to treat sexual desire disorders, masturbation must have this particular relationship with sexual desire and sexual activity. In this case, masturbation should influence sexual desire, which should lead to dyadic sexual activity.

In addition, this study sought to extend the previous literature by examining the relationship between masturbation and other constructs: overall sexual dysfunction, relationship satisfaction, life stress, and sex-

FIGURE 1. A Conceptual Illustration of the Hypotheses

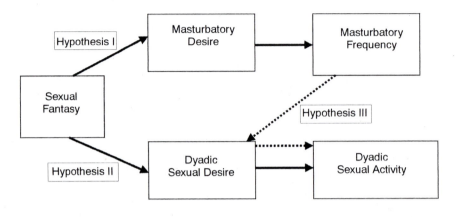

ual activity. Relationship satisfaction was measured because masturbation may result from decreased relationship satisfaction (Reading & Wiest, 1984). Life stress was assessed because masturbation is sometimes viewed as a way to release tension (see Laumann et al., 1994). Differences in masturbation by sex, relationship status, racial/ethnic group status, and religious affiliation were also examined.

METHOD

Participants in this study were 549 volunteer college students at a Midwestern university. Participants were tested individually and in small groups of 2-15. Consent forms were distributed and collected before the questionnaire packets were administered to protect the participant's anonymity. Most respondents completed the questionnaire packet within one hour. Each participant received a written debriefing form and class credit for his/her participation. The targeted number of participants was based upon a power analysis in which power = .80, alpha = .01, and effect size = medium (Cohen, 1992).

Participants

Of the 549 participants completing the surveys, six were discarded because of incomplete data. The remaining sample of 543 predominantly consisted of individuals who were female (63.7%), young (mean age = 18.58 years), heterosexual (91.7%), European-American (60%), Catholic (60%), and in their first year of college (73.7%). The frequency of attending religious services varied, with 27.8% attending once or a few times in the past year, 27.8% attending once or a few times each month, and 30.6% attending services at least weekly.

Most respondents were single (41%), but several reported they were in a non-married committed relationship (35%). The majority (75%) had engaged in some type of sexual activity (e.g., vaginal, oral, or anal intercourse) in their lifetime. Most participants (28.2%) indicated they had experienced one emotionally significant romantic or sexual relationship in their lifetime, with 22.8% reporting two such relationships and 15.8% reporting no such relationships.

Measures

Participants were asked to complete a questionnaire packet which included a demographics questionnaire that assessed each individual's race/ethnicity, religious affiliation, frequency of attending religious services, and relationship status. In addition, respondents were administered a questionnaire packet containing the following measures:

The 25-item Hurlbert Index of Sexual Desire (Apt & Hurlbert, 1992) asks participants to indicate how often (1 = All the time to 5 = Never) a given statement describes them (e.g., "I look forward to having sex with my partner"). A mean total score was used for this study, with possible scores ranging from 1 to 5. Higher scores indicate higher levels of sexual desire.

The Sexual Desire Inventory (SDI; Spector, Carey, & Steinberg, 1996) consists of two subscales that assess one's desire to engage in sexual activity alone (i.e., masturbation) and with a partner. Respondents indicate their level of sexual desire and frequency of desire using an 8 or 9 point Likert-type scale (e.g., 0 = No Desire to 8 = Strong Desire). The Masturbation subscale includes three items and the Dyadic subscale includes eight items. For both subscales, total scores are based on a sum of the items, and higher scores indicate higher levels of sexual desire.

The Hurlbert Index of Sexual Fantasy (Hurlbert & Apt, 1993) is a 25-item scale assessing the degree to which an individual engages in sexual fantasy. Participants indicate how often (1 = All the time to 5 = Never) a given statement describes them (e.g., "I feel guilty about my sexual fantasies"). The total score can be calculated by summing the items. Higher scores indicate a higher level of sexual fantasy.

The Sexual Boredom Scale (Watt & Ewing, 1996) measures the degree to which an individual tends to experience boredom with sexual activity. Respondents indicate the degree to which 18 statements describes them (e.g., "I frequently find it difficult to sustain my sexual interest in a relationship") using a 7-point Likert-type scale (1 = Highly disagree to 7 = Highly Agree). Total scores are based on a mean of all items and range from 1 to 7, with higher scores indicating greater levels of sexual boredom.

The 30-item Sexuality Scale (Snell & Papini, 1988) assesses sexual depression (i.e., feeling depressed about the sexual aspects of one's life), sexual self-esteem, and sexual preoccupation (i.e., thinking about sex). Each subscale consists of 10 items. Participants indicate how well (1 = Agree to 5 = Disagree) a statement describes them (e.g., "Engaging in group sex is an entertaining idea"). Each total score equals a mean of the relevant items. Higher scores reflect greater levels of each construct.

The Sexual Opinion Survey (SOS; Fisher, Byrne, White, & Kelley, 1988) measures the degree of erotophobia-erotophilia (Cronbach's alpha = .88 for males and .90 for females). Participants indicate their degree of agreement with 21 statements about sexuality (e.g., "Masturbation can be an exciting experience") using a 7-point Likert scale (from 1 = I strongly agree to 7 = I strongly disagree). Scores range from 0 to 126. Low scores indicate that an individual has negative emotional responses to sexual matters (erotophobia) and high scores reflect positive emotional responses to sexual matters (erotophilia).

The Relationship Assessment Scale (Hendrick, 1988) consists of 7 items on a 5-point Likert-type scale. This scale assesses general satisfaction with aspects of a person's romantic relationship (e.g., "How much do you love your partner?"). A mean score represents the total score, and higher scores reflect greater satisfaction.

The Index of Sexual Satisfaction (Hudson, Harrison, & Crosscup, 1981) measures level of satisfaction with respect the sexual aspects of one's romantic relationship. Respondents indicate the degree to which 25 statements (e.g., "I feel that my partner enjoys our sex life") describes them using a 5-point Likert-type scale (1 = rarely or none of the time to 5 = Most or all of the time). Total scores are based on a mean of all items and range from 1 to 5, with higher scores indicating greater levels of sexual dissatisfaction.

The Life Events Scale for Students is a 36-item measure of life stress (Clements & Turpin, 1996). Respondents indicate whether or not they have experienced a given event (e.g., death of a parent, break-up with a partner) in their lifetime. Total scores are calculated by multiplying each experienced event by a weight to account for the event's severity and summing these products. Scores range from 0 to 100. Higher scores indicate higher levels of stress.

The 20-item short form of the Marlowe-Crowne Social Desirability Scale (MCSDS; Strahan & Gerbasi, 1972) measures the tendency of participants to give socially desirable responses (Kuder-Richardson ranges from .78 to .87). Participants read statements and indicate whether the item is true or false as it pertains to their personality (e.g., "I like to gossip at times"). Scores range from 0 to 20, and higher scores correspond to the tendency to provide socially correct answers.

Participants were asked how often they had masturbated in the past 12 months (0 = Never to 10 = More than Once a Day) and their number of lifetime male and female sexual partners (i.e., a total number of life-time sexual partners). Participants were asked to indicate how often they had engaged in coitus, oral sex (giving and receiving), and anal in-tercourse during their lifetime, considering all of their sexual partners (e.g., A = Never, B = Not often, 1-2 times, E = Quite Frequently, more than 10 times). The five options were assigned a weight (i.e., from 0-4) and the numbers were summed for a total score. Scores could range from 0-16, with higher scores reflecting greater levels of sexual activ-ity. To briefly assess sexual dysfunction, participants checked any sex-ual difficulties they have experienced in the following areas: orgasmic, arousal, sexual desire, pain, vaginal muscles spasms, or premature ejac-ulation. Scores range from 0-5, with higher numbers indicating more sexual dysfunction.

RESULTS

Because of the high number of analyses conducted, a conservative significance level of alpha = .01 was used. Each measure's internal reli-ability was determined by calculating Cronbach's alphas, all of which were adequate (Cronbach's alpha ranged from .70 to .94).

A multivariate analysis of covariance (MANCOVA) was employed to examine differences in masturbatory desire (i.e., a subscale of the SDI) and masturbatory frequency (i.e., self-report in the past 12 months). These two dependent variables were adequately correlated ($r = .83$, $p = .00$) to be included in the analysis together. Because social desirability was modestly but significantly correlated with masturbatory desire ($r = -.11$, $p = .01$) and masturbatory frequency ($r = -.12$, $p = .004$), social desirability was used as a covariate. The independent variables included sex (male versus female), race/ethnicity (European-American versus non-European-American), religious affiliation (Catholic versus non-Catholic), relationship status (single versus non-single), and year in school (first year versus non-first years). The overall MANCOVA was significant, $F = 5.32$ (2,500) $p = .005$. Univariate analyses indicate that there was a significant effect for gender, $F = 70.45$ (2,500) $p = .000$. Men reported higher levels of masturbatory desire and greater levels of masturbatory frequency when compared to women (see Table 1). A significant main effect of race was also evident, $F = 4.83$ (2,500) $p = .008$. European-American participants reported higher levels of masturbatory desire and greater levels of masturbatory frequency when compared to non-European-American participants (see Table 1). There was not a significant main effect for relationship status, year in school, or religious affiliation. A post-hoc correlation was computed between religious attendance and masturbation. Lower levels of attendance at religious services was significantly associated with higher levels of masturbatory desire ($r = .14$, $p = .00$) and frequency ($r = .14$, $p = .00$).

To examine the race/ethnicity findings more closely, ANOVAs were conducted without collapsing across racial/ethnic groups. The five levels of the independent variables included African-Americans, European-Americans, Latinos, Asian-Americans, and unclassified persons. The analysis with masturbatory frequency was significant, $F = 4.61$ (4,525) $p = .001$. Follow-up Tukey tests indicated that African-American and Latino participants each reported masturbating less often than European-American participants (see Table 1). The analysis with masturbatory desire was also significant, $F = 5.86$ (4,532) $p = .0001$. Follow-up Tukey tests indicated that African-American, Latino, and Asian-American groups of participants each reported lower levels of masturbatory desire compared to European-Americans (see Table 1). A post-hoc ANOVA revealed that Asian-American and Latino participants had significantly more conservative sexual attitudes compared to European-Americans, $F = 8.33$ (3,495) $p = .0000$ (see Table 1).

Correlates of Masturbatory Desire and Frequency

Correlations were computed between the two masturbation measures and the various instruments. When the correlations were examined by

TABLE 1. Means and Standard Deviations for Gender and Ethnic Groups

	Masturbatory Frequency	Masturbatory Desire	Sexual Attitudes
Males (N = 195)	5.91 (2.75)	9.62 (6.24)	---
Females (N = 339)	2.15 (2.45)*	3.47 (5.13)*	---
Caucasian (N = 325)	3.97 (3.16)	6.70 (6.42)	---
Non-Caucasian (N = 209)	2.83 (2.98)*	4.17 (5.78)*	---
African-American (N = 33)	2.36 (2.68)*	3.39 (5.83)*	64.94 (20.97)
Asian-American (N = 75)	2.95 (3.14)	4.21 (5.57)*	57.76 (22.50)*
European-American (N = 325)	3.97 (3.16)	6.70 (6.42)	70.18 (21.50)
Latino/a (N = 57)	2.72 (2.82)*	3.79 (5.72)*	61.65 (23.65)*
Unclassified (N = 40)	3.15 (3.13)	5.28 (6.08)	67.03 (21.59)

Note: The sum of Ns do not always equal 543 due to missing data. Means with an "*" are significantly different compared to the male, Caucasian, or European-American groups. Range of possible scores: 0-10 for masturbatory frequency, 0-23 for masturbatory desire, and 0-126 for sexual attitudes. Higher scores = greater frequency, more desire, and more positive attitudes. Standard deviations are in parentheses.

gender, the pattern of results was the same. Thus, males and females were combined in the analyses. For significant correlations, forward multiple regression analyses were conducted to determine the best predictors of masturbatory desire and frequency. Social desirability was covaried in the regression analyses.

Several measures were not significantly correlated with masturbatory desire or frequency (see Table 2): sexual depression, sexual self-esteem, and general as well as sexual satisfaction in a relationship. (Only participants currently in a relationship were included for the latter correlations.) Two trends were evident: higher levels of sexual depression were marginally associated with higher levels of masturbatory desire, and higher levels of masturbatory frequency were marginally associated with lower levels of relationship satisfaction (see Table 2). Masturbatory frequency and desire were significantly correlated with life stress, with greater frequency and desire being associated with more life stress.

TABLE 2. Correlations Between the Protocol Measures and Masturbatory Frequency and Desire

	Sexual Depression	Sexual Self-Esteem	Life Stress	Relationship^ Satisfaction	Sexual^ Satisfaction
FREQ.	.06	.11*	.13**	−.12[a]	−.02
DESIRE	.10*	.06	.16***	−.06	−.02

	Sexual Partners	Sexual Boredom	Life Sex	Relationship^ Dysfunction	Sexual^ Attitudes
FREQ.	.08	.14**	.17***	.08	.59 ***
DESIRE	.09[a]	.13**	.11**	.09[a]	.59 ***

	Hurlbert Index Sexual Desire	Hurlbert Index Sexual Fantasy	Sexual Preoccupation	Sexual Desire Inventory
FREQ.	.44 ***	.43 ***	.50 ***	.42 ***
DESIRE	.41 ***	.40 ***	.49 ***	.43 ***

Note: [a]$p < .05$ *$p < .02$ **$p < .01$ ***$p < .001$. FREQ = masturbatory frequency. DESIRE = masturbatory desire. The '^' indicates that only participants currently in a relationship were included.

Correlations were also computed between the masturbation measures and other indices of sexual behavior. The masturbation measures were significantly correlated with lifetime sexual activity and sexual boredom, but not with number of lifetime sex partners or sexual dysfunction (see Table 2). Higher levels of masturbatory desire and frequency were associated with greater levels of sexual boredom and lifetime sexual activity.

The masturbation measures were significantly correlated with the Sexual Desire Inventory (SDI), Hurlbert Index of Sexual Desire (HISD), Hurlbert Index of Sexual Fantasy (HISF), sexual preoccupation scale (i.e., a type of sexual fantasy instrument), and sexual attitudes measure (see Table 2). High levels of masturbatory desire and frequency were associated with high levels of sexual desire and fantasy.

Regression Analyses

The two dyadic sexual desire measures (i.e., the SDI and HISD) and two sexual fantasy measures (i.e., the HISF and sexual preoccupation scale) are conceptually similar and were highly correlated. This suggests that two conceptually similar scales would compete for the same variance in a regression analysis involving multiple predictors; thus, forward multiple regression analyses were employed to determine which sexual desire measure and which sexual fantasy scale were better predictors of the masturbation measures for future regression analyses. The HISD measure and the sexual preoccupation were each better predictors.

A forward multiple regression analysis was conducted in which the key constructs from the prior correlational analyses were combined to determine the best predictor of masturbatory desire and frequency. The independent variables in these analyses included lifetime stress, sexual boredom, sexual desire, lifetime sexual activity, sexual attitudes, and sexual preoccupation. The sexual attitudes measure was the best predictor of masturbatory desire, with sexual preoccupation and lifetime sexual activity accounting for a significant amount of additional variance; lifetime stress was a marginal predictor (see Table 3). Together, these four predictors accounted for 42.10% of the variance in masturbatory desire, F (533,5) = 75.34, p = .000. Sexual desire and sexual boredom were not significant predictors. The second regression analysis revealed similar results. Sexual attitudes best predicted masturbatory frequency, with sexual preoccupation accounting for a significant amount of additional variance. Lifetime sexual activity and sexual desire accounted for a marginally significant amount of additional variance (see Table 3). Together, these four predictors accounted for 39.37% of the variance in masturbatory desire, F (533,5) = 67.15, p = .000. Lifetime stress and sexual boredom were not significant predictors.

Analyses of Mediation

A stepwise multiple regression was conducted to examine Hypothesis I, the hypothesis that desire for masturbation mediates the relationship between sexual preoccupation and masturbatory frequency. To test for a mediator, the relationship between the independent variable and the dependent variable is examined after the mediating variable is removed (Baron & Kenny, 1986; Holmbeck, 1997). Prior correlations have already shown that sexual preoccupation is significantly associated with masturbatory desire and frequency (see Table 2) and that the two masturbation measures are significantly correlated with each other, satisfying the initial requirements of a mediator test (Baron & Kenny, 1986). When masturbatory desire is covaried, sexual preoccupation still significantly predicts masturbatory frequency (p = .000), but there is a significant drop in the beta-weight associated with sexual preoccupation (Baron & Kenny, 1986). The original beta-weight of .502 drops to

TABLE 3. Forward Regression Analyses with Predictors of Masturbatory Desire and Frequency

	Step	R^2	F	SigF	B	SE B	β	SigFCh
Masturbatory Desire								
social desirability	1	.0103	5.441	.020	.1166	.0593	.0700	
sexual attitudes	2	.3575	144.967	.000	.1433	.0131	.5036	.0000
sexual preoccupation	3	.3961	113.711	.000	.1528	.0328	.2204	.0000
lifetime sexual activity	4	.4170	92.813	.000	−.2223	.0468	−.1787	.0000
lifetime stress	5	.4210	75.340	.000	.0019	.0009	.0678	.0586
sexual desire (HISD)	6	.4238	63.380	.000	.0271	.0183	.0700	.1149
sexual boredom	7	.4239	54.245	.000	−.0742	.2391	−.0112	.7564
	Step	R^2	F	SigF	B	SE B	β	SigFCh
Masturbatory Frequency								
social desirability	1	.0148	7.820	.005	.0323	.0305	.0388	
sexual attitudes	2	.3420	135.133	.000	.0638	.0067	.4776	.0000
sexual preoccupation	3	.3826	107.214	.000	.0706	.0169	.2033	.0000
lifetime sexual activity	4	.3883	82.199	.000	−.0629	.0240	−.1010	.0289
sexual desire (HISD)	5	.3937	67.154	.000	.0207	.0094	.1069	.0314
lifetime stress	6	.3943	55.993	.000	.0003	.0005	.0250	.4763
sexual boredom	7	.3945	47.929	.000	.0424	.1228	.0128	.7300

Note: SigF = significance of F. SigFCh = significance of F change.

.124. A mediational effect is evident, but because the relationship remains significant, partial mediation has been demonstrated (Baron & Kenny, 1986).

A second stepwise multiple regression was conducted to examine Hypothesis II, the hypothesis that dyadic sexual desire mediates the relationship between sexual fantasy and lifetime sexual activity. Sexual activity is correlated with sexual preoccupation ($r = .15, p = .003$), the measure of sexual fantasy. Sexual desire is correlated with lifetime sexual activity ($r = .28, p = .000$) and with the sexual preoccupation measure ($r = .60, p = .000$). When sexual desire is covaried, sexual preoccupation does not significantly predict sexual activity ($p = .646$), and there a significant drop in the beta-weight associated with sexual preoccupation. The original beta-weight of .247 drops to .024, a full mediational effect is evident (Baron & Kenny, 1986).

A third stepwise multiple regression was conducted to examine Hypothesis III, the hypothesis that dyadic sexual desire mediates the relationship between masturbatory frequency and dyadic sexual activity. Prior correlations have shown that masturbatory frequency was correlated with sexual desire and lifetime sexual activity (see Table 2). Sexual desire and sexual activity are also correlated ($r = .28$, $p = .000$). When sexual desire is covaried, masturbatory frequency does not significantly predict sexual activity ($p = .993$), and there, a significant drop in the beta-weight associated with masturbatory frequency. The original beta-weight of .174 drops to zero. A full mediational effect is evident (Baron & Kenny, 1986).

DISCUSSION

Male participants reported higher levels of masturbatory desire and frequency than their female counterparts, a finding that has been consistently shown in prior research (e.g., Oliver & Hyde, 1993). This study also provided support for the notion that European Americans have higher levels of masturbatory desire and frequency when compared to non-European Americans. This may result from more conservative sexual scripts among minority ethnic/racial groups that emphasize penile-vaginal intercourse rather than other forms of sexual expression (e.g., Laumann et al., 1994). This notion is supported by the finding that some non-European American participants in this study had more conservative sexual attitudes than European Americans.

No differences were found in masturbatory desire or frequency with respect to religious affiliation. Yet, religious attendance showed a modest but significant correlation with masturbatory desire and frequency. Religious attendance may be a more critical factor than religious affiliation when examining relationships between sexuality and religion, which has been shown in prior research (Davidson et al., 1995). People who consistently attend religious services may be more apt to share conservative views toward sexuality espoused by their denominations.

No differences in masturbatory desire or frequency were evident based on relationship status. These results suggest that masturbatory desire and frequency are independent of relationship status. For individuals in a committed relationship, however, higher levels of general relationship dissatisfaction were associated with higher levels of masturbatory frequency. Similar results have been reported elsewhere (Reading & Wiest, 1984). When dissatisfaction in a relationship increases, one or both partners may be less willing to initiate or consent to dyadic sexual activity. Thus, sexual fantasies lead to masturbatory desire and increases in masturbatory activity. Longitudinal studies are needed to help examine whether or not masturbatory frequency increases as the result of decreased relationship satisfaction and dyadic sexual activity. The fact that higher levels of life stress were significantly associated with higher levels of masturbatory desire and frequency support the idea that people masturbate to relax themselves (Laumann et al., 1994).

The positive relationships between sexual boredom, lifetime sexual activity, masturbatory desire, and masturbatory frequency are intriguing. People with high levels of sexual boredom may have higher levels of masturbatory desire and frequency because they have a higher sex drive and would like greater sexual stimulation. The result that both masturbatory desire and frequency were significantly associated with sexual boredom suggests that sexually bored individuals may utilize masturbation to augment their sexual experiences to enhance their overall sexual fulfillment. High levels of lifetime sexual activity may be associated with high levels of masturbatory sexual desire and frequency again because some people have higher levels of sexual desire. Rather than consistently seek dyadic sexual activity, people with higher levels of sexual desire choose to masturbate. Masturbation could also serve as an outlet that prevents individuals from seeking sexual activity outside their primary relationship.

Overall sexual dysfunction levels were not related to masturbatory frequency, suggesting that masturbation does not lead to fewer sexual problems. This finding has been previously documented by Leitenberg et al. (1993), but both the current study and the Leitenberg study employed broad measures of sexual dysfunction. Such broad measures may make it difficult to pinpoint specific benefits of masturbation in lifetime sexual functioning. More detailed studies are needed to assess the relationship between masturbation and later sexual problems. For instance, women who masturbate as adolescents may experience better orgasms and may be less likely to experience pain during coitus, especially during first coitus. Thus, specific questions should assess the following: age at first orgasm, frequency of orgasms, degree of enjoyment of orgasms, frequency of unwanted pain during intercourse. These are example questions that future studies need to include when examining the relationship between masturbation and sexual dysfunction or difficulties. Such a study is currently underway by the first author.

The results of this study support the use of masturbation to treat HSDD. Masturbatory desire and frequency appear to have close relationships with sexual thoughts (i.e., the sexual preoccupation scale), sexual fantasies, and sexual desire. Sexual fantasies may have been such a strong predictor of masturbatory desire and frequency because of its apparent generative role in sexual functioning. Causal inferences cannot be made from this study, but the mediational analysis suggests that sexual thoughts (fantasies) lead to masturbatory desire which in turn leads to masturbation. The other hypothesized pathways appear to have been supported. Sexual fantasy influences sexual desire, which in turn leads to sexual activity. In addition, masturbatory activity appears to influence sexual desire, which in turn influences dyadic sexual activity. This finding supports the notion that masturbation may be useful in treating individuals who have HSDD. Masturbation may allow individuals to gain greater familiarity with their bodies and sexual responses, leading to more consistent orgasms and a desire for dyadic sexual activity (see Hurlbert, 1993). Thus, therapists may find guided masturbation exercises useful in treating HSDD. Of course, this assumes masturbation is an acceptable, fulfilling activity that can lead to orgasm for clients. Given that sexual attitudes appears to be the best predictor of masturbatory desire and frequency (Kelly et al., 1990), therapists will want to encourage positive attitudes toward masturbation for this intervention to work. These analyses represent initial steps in illustrating the potential causal mechanisms between masturbation, sexual fantasy, sexual desire and sexual activity.

This study is limited by its use of a convenience sample. The results may not be generalizable to individuals who are seeking treatment for sexual dysfunctions. Nonetheless, this study represents an important first step in developing a model of masturbation that illustrates its role in sexual functioning and highlights its potential role in sex therapy.

REFERENCES

Apt, C. V., & Hurlbert, D. F. (1992). Motherhood and female sexuality beyond one year postpartum: A study of military wives. *Journal of Sex Education and Therapy, 18*, 104-114.

American Psychiatric Association. (1994). Diagnostic and statistical manual of mental disorders (4th ed.). Washington, DC: Author.

Beck, J. G. (1995). Hypoactive sexual desire disorder: An overview. *Journal of Consulting and Clinical Psychology, 63,* 919-927.

Baron, R. M., & Kenny, D. A. (1986). The moderator-mediator variable distinction in social psychological research: Conceptual, strategic, and statistical considerations. *Journal of Personality and Social Psychology, 51,* 1173-1182.

Campagna, A. F. (1985-86). Fantasy and sexual arousal in college men: Normative and functional aspects. *Imagination, Cognition, & Personality, 5,* 3-20.

Clements, K., & Turpin, G. (1996). The life events scale for students: Validation for use with British samples. *Personality and Individual Differences, 20,* 747-751.

Davidson, J. K., Darling, C. A., & Norton, L. (1996). Religiosity and the sexuality of women: Sexual behavior and sexual satisfaction revisited. *Journal of Sex Research, 32,* 235-243.

Donahey, K. M., & Carroll, R. A. (1993). Gender differences in factors associated with hypoactive sexual desire. *Journal of Sex and Marital Therapy, 19,* 25-40.

Fisher, W. A., Byrne, D., White, L. A., & Kelley, K. (1988). Erotophobia-erotophilia as a dimension of personality. *The Journal of Sex Research, 25,* 123-151.

Hendrick, S. S. (1988). A generic measure of relationship satisfaction. *Journal of Marriage and the Family, 50,* 93-98.

Holmbeck, G. N. (1997). Toward terminological, conceptual, and statistical clarity in the study of mediators and moderators: Examples from the child-clinical and pediatric psychology literatures. *Journal of Consulting and Clinical Psychology, 65,* 599-610.

Hudson, W. W., Harrison, D. F., & Crosscup, P. C. (1981). A short-form scale to measure sexual discord in dyadic relationships. *The Journal of Sex Research, 17,* 157-174.

Hurlbert, D. F. (1993). A comparative study using orgasm consistency training in the treatment of women reporting hypoactive sexual desire. *Journal of Sex and Marital Therapy, 19,* 41-55.

Hurlbert, D. F., & Apt, C. (1993). Female sexuality: A comparative study between women in homosexual and heterosexual relationships. *Journal of Sex and Marital Therapy, 19,* 315-327.

Hurlbert, D. F., & Apt, C. (1995). The coital alignment technique and directed masturbation: A comparative study on female orgasm. *Journal of Sex and Marital Therapy, 21,* 21-29.

Hurlbert, D. F., & Whittaker, K. E. (1991). The role of masturbation in marital and sexual satisfaction: A comparative study of female masturbators and nonmasturbators. *Journal of Sex Education and Therapy, 17,* 272-282.

Jones, J. C., & Barlow, D. H. (1990). Self-reported frequency of sexual urges, fantasies, and masturbatory fantasies in heterosexual males and females. *Archives of Sexual Behavior, 19,* 269-279.

Kelly, M. P., Strassberg, D. S., & Kircher, J. R. (1990). Attitudinal and experiential correlates of anorgasmia. *Archives of Sexual Behavior, 19,* 165-177.

Kolodny, R. C. (1981). Evaluating sex therapy: Process and outcome at the Masters & Johnson Institute. *Journal of Sex Research, 17,* 301-318.

Laumann, E. O., Gagnon, J. H., Michael, R. T., & Michaels, S. (1994). The social organization of sexuality: Sexual practices in the United States. Chicago: University of Chicago Press.

Leitenberg, H., Detzer, M. J., & Srebnik, D. (1993). Gender difference sin masturbation and the relation of masturbation experience in preadolescence and/or early adolescence to sexual behavior and sexual adjustment in young adulthood. *Archives of
Sexual Behavior, 22,* 87-98.

Meston, C. M., Trapnell, P. D., & Gorzalka, B. B. (1996). Ethnic and gender differences in sexuality: Variations in sexual behavior between Asian and non-Asian university students. *Archives of Sexual Behavior, 25,* 33-72.

Nutter, D. E., & Condron, M. K. (1985). Sexual fantasy and activity patterns of males
with inhibited sexual desire and males with erectile dysfunction versus normal con-
trols. *Journal of Sex & Marital Therapy, 11,* 91-98.

Oliver, M. B., & Hyde, J. S. (1993). Gender differences in sexuality: A meta-analysis.
Psychological Bulletin, 114, 29-51.

Patton, M. S. (1985). Masturbation from Judaism to Victorianism. *Journal of Religion
& Health, 24,* 133-146.

Pelletier, L. A., & Herold, E. S. (1989). The relationship of age, sex guilt, and sexual
experience with female sexual fantasies. *Journal of Sex Research, 24,* 250-256.

Reading, A. E., & Wiest, W. M. (1984). An analysis of self-reported sexual behavior in
a sample of normal males. *Archives of Sexual Behavior, 13,* 69-83.

Renshaw, D. C. (1981). A modern view of ancient taboos–masturbation, oral sex, and
anal sex. *Consultant, 21,* 207-212.

Rosen, R. C., & Leiblum, S. R. (1995). Hypoactive sexual desire. *The Psychiatric
Clinics of North America, 18,* 107-121.

Snell, W. E., & Papini, D. R. (1988). The sexuality scale: An instrument to measure
sexual-esteem, sexual-depression, and sexual-preoccupation.

Spector, I. L., Carey, M. P., & Steinberg, L. (1996). The sexual desire inventory: Development, factor structure, and evidence of reliability. *Journal of Sex and Marital
Therapy, 22,* 175-190.

Strahan, R., & Gerbasi, K. C. (1972). Short, homogenous versions of the Marlowe-
Crowne social desirability scale. *Journal of Clinical Psychology, 28,* 191-193.

Watt, J. D., & Ewing, J. E. (1996). Toward the development and validation of a measure of sexual boredom. *The Journal of Sex Research, 33,* 57-66.

Index